SAFE AT HOME

a memoir

Orson Bean

BALBOA
PRESS
A DIVISION OF HAY HOUSE

Balboa Press books may be ordered through booksellers or by contacting:

Balboa Press
A Division of Hay House
1663 Liberty Drive
Bloomington, IN 47403
www.balboapress.com
1-(877) 407-4847

Printed in the United States of America.

ISBN: 978-1-4525-7528-5 (sc)
ISBN: 978-1-4525-7529-2 (e)

Library of Congress Control Number: 2013910093

Balboa Press rev. date: 6/11/2013

For my dearest Alley

Who put up with a lot while I was writing it

When I take communion (ritualized cannibalism) tears come to my eyes. This happens because during that rite I remember that the two thousand year old man (sorry Mel Brooks) whom I believe (in some way I can't explain) to be the Son of God (Whom I also can't explain) instructed His followers (one of whom I have become) to symbolically drink His blood (sorry Bela Lugosi) and eat His body (sorry Jeffrey Daumer) and by doing so to become a part of Him. I find that deeply moving.

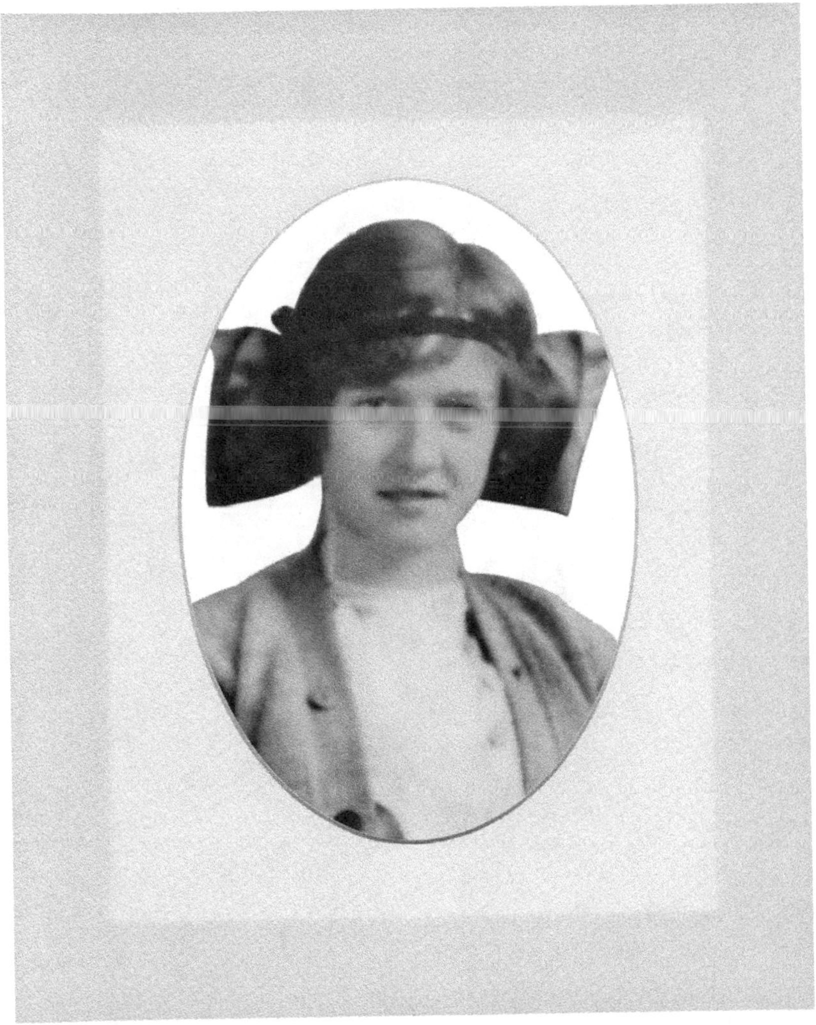

I

The year was 1938 and I was ten. My mother was sitting at the kitchen table and I was standing in the doorway to the pantry. A glass of sherry, an ashtray, and a pack of Kools sat next to her on the oil-cloth covered table. She held a cigarette in one hand and a can opener in the other. It was one of the new ones which had only recently appeared on the market, a brand new innovative technology in the opening of cans. It had porcelain handles with the word Lund inscribed on one of them.

"He asked me to marry him, you know." she said.

"Who did?"

"Mr. Lund. Eddie. Eddie Lund was his name. We went to college together. Well, he was a year older than I was, but I knew him. Then he asked me out and we dated for a while. He was crazy about me. So in love, he said. And he asked me to marry him but I said no. I just didn't love him and without love, you know... I mean love makes the world go 'round." She pause for a moment and then went on. "But I had no idea of what he was going to accomplish. I mean, look at this..." She held up the can opener. "He's made millions off it and more to come."

I stared at her. She had a habit of talking to me as if I were one of her girl friends; someone she knew well enough to confide in. "But if you'd married him, you wouldn't have had me."

She gazed at the can opener in her hand and didn't answer for a while. When she finally did, she said, "Yes… well…" and her voice trailed off as she seemed to think about something else. Then, she reached for her glass and took another sip of wine.

———•———

I loved my mother to distraction. To me she was the most beautiful woman on earth. And in actual fact, I wasn't far off in my assessment. She was strikingly beautiful and overtly sexual and funny as hell, and she loved my father as much as I loved her. Loved him so much, was so infatuated with him, so obsessed with him that there was no love left over for me. It has been said that there is no greater aphrodisiac than indifference. Men follow women across continents because the women are not particularly interested in them. That was the way my mother felt about me: not particularly interested. And I would indeed have followed her across continents.

She did, however, entrust me with a job of enormous importance: keeping her alive. Marian Pollard Burrows, who had luxurious auburn hair, eyes of the darkest brown, a perfect nose and a slim figure with breasts to make Titian weep, lacked one thing: any sense of self worth. Men stopped in their tracks to stare at her; she took it for granted. People howled with laughter at her wit; she attached no importance to it. She had a son who worshipped her; she barely noticed it. The one thing that mattered to her was her husband.

"If he ever leaves me, I'll kill myself," she had said to me, one day shortly after I had turned six. "If you want me to stay alive it's your job to keep him around." I understood that she meant what she said, and with a silent "aye, aye", I chose to accept the mission. I would convince my rival for my mother's affection that I, his son, loved him more than anything in the world. That way, I reasoned, my father would be disinclined to leave hearth and home and my mother would not kill herself. Rarely had a six year old boy been given such a job or taken it on with such zeal. And for quite a long time it worked.

————•————

George Burrows was a man of extraordinary intelligence. His brilliance, however, never translated into the ability to make a living of any consequence. He drifted from one job to another. He assumed, for a year, the position of president of the Community Church of Boston, a house of worship more concerned with progressive politics than with a Supreme Being. He helped found the New England branch of the A.C.L.U., and became active with causes like the abolition of the death penalty, and justice for Negroes. Never once did he take me out and teach me how to throw and catch a ball. It was obvious to my father that I adored him, and that more or less took care of his parental obligations.

He had been a law student, back when he met my mother. He had read about her in The Boston Globe. Her comings and goings were catalogued in the rotogravure section; she was a second cousin to the then president Calvin Coolidge. She had visited "Cousin Cal" in the White House and enjoyed a stay of several months. With her beauty and wit she had captivated the capitol. Back in Boston, she had run into him at a meeting of some kind and he, like everyone else in the room, had been unable to take his eyes off her. A penniless student, he had summoned up the courage to speak to her. She found him fascinating. He spoke to her of politics and the unfairness of life for the downtrodden. She came from Perkinsville, Vermont; he was a man of the world. He swept her off her feet and into his bed and in time they were married.

I was born in July, 1928, in Burlington, Vermont. It was the last year of Calvin Coolidge's presidency. My mother and father's marriage had taken place seven months earlier, and she had gone to Vermont to stay with her parents and have the baby. Her father was called Dallas and she named me after him. He had been named after President Polk's vice president. Who would name their kid after an obscure president's even more obscure vice president? My grandfather's parents did and my mother did the same, so I suffered from the name throughout my childhood.

My father had interrupted his law studies to take a job "down south" in Atlanta, Georgia, looking after a cerebral palsied young man named Jack Fields. "The family is Jewish but quite nice," he wrote to his wife. The pay was minimal but times were tough and he was glad to have a job, any job to begin to support his fledgling family. They were apart for almost half a year. When I was only three months old, my mother and grandparents took me to the White House, where "Cousin Cal" held me in his arms. When asked about it later, I couldn't recall the president's having said anything to me.

As soon as my father had saved up enough money to afford the rent on a small apartment in the Boston area, he sent for his new wife and son. The place he'd found was in Watertown. We didn't stay there long; too many Armenians, he said. He got a job selling socks in Filene's Basement and the family moved to an apartment in Cambridge. After a short while, we moved again. He had acquired work as an insurance adjustor for the New Amsterdam Casualty Company. This meant that when one of their clients had a car accident, the company sent him to look at the damage and report how much money, if any, they should spend to repair the vehicle. The pay was better than what he had received at Filene's, so we were now living in a somewhat more genteel Cambridge neighborhood.

My parents rented the bottom half of a house which looked out on a city reservoir called Fresh Pond, so that was where my mother told people we lived: on Fresh Pond. My father would take the subway home from Boston after work every day to the end of the line in Harvard Square. There, he would switch to a streetcar which came up out of the ground just north of the square, and carried him, twenty five minutes later, to within walking distance of our home. He kept a faded copy of the Boston Transcript in his desk. It featured an article about the days when the subway was extended past Central Square to Harvard Square. A kiosk with entrances and exits to the station had been put up in the middle of the square, and the university staff had objected to it on aesthetic grounds. The headline of the piece read "Harvard President Fights Erection in Square."

Sometimes my father would bring home live crabs, which my mother would drop into a pot of boiling water on the stove. When they had turned red, we would eat the crabs, retrieving the meat with nutcrackers and little picks which normally would be used to pry filberts and cashews out of their shells. On other days he would come home with a coconut. Using an ice pick and hammer, he would open the three holes at the top of the coconut, drain out the little bit of sweet milk, and I would be allowed to drink some of it. Then he would smash the coconut apart and we would all share the coconut meat.

The landlady, Mrs. Anastos, lived upstairs. She had a son named Tyke, who had a dog. There was a back yard to the house with a little copse of pine trees in it. I liked to play among the trees with Tyke and his dog. One day the play became overly exuberant, and the dog bit me on the face. The doctor came to the house and stitched me up while my parents held me down on the kitchen table and I screamed. Mrs. Anastos explained that the dog had never bitten anyone before, her apology was accepted, and I was admonished to be more careful in the future.

Those were the halcyon days; my mother had not yet begun to drink. After my father had left for work in the morning, she would take me by streetcar and subway into Boston. I was five and had not yet been enrolled in school. We'd go to the movies and I'd sit close to her in the darkened theater. "Don't tell your father," she'd whisper. It was conspiratorial and exciting. I'd lean my head against her arm, and smell her perfume. Sometimes we'd do a double feature (movies were only an hour and a quarter long in those days), and have a bite in between at the counter in the Five and Ten, where a hot turkey sandwich, with mashed potatoes served from an ice cream scoop, was twenty cents. When we got home, she would hurriedly trot out the dry floor mop and tidy up the house. "Don't mention our date," she'd remind me.

George Burrow's boss at the New Amsterdam Casualty Company was, he would complain, a tyrant who gave him nothing but trouble. His name was Mr. Rice. When my father would come home tired from his day's work and grumble about Mr. Rice, I would tell him that I would go to the office myself, and call the boss Riced Potatoes! It always made my mother and father laugh. The day my father lost his job, it was Mr. Rice who delivered the news. He didn't arrive home until after midnight. To save the nickel subway fare he had walked all the way from Boston.

II

The family downsized to a working class Irish Catholic neighborhood in North Cambridge. My mother's people had helped out for a while, but the aid ceased to arrive when their son-in-law applied for work with the W.P.A. That was the last straw for the Pollards, who were ardent Republicans. But the job application paid off. George Burrow's intellectual abilities were off the chart by W.P.A. standards, and he was offered work evaluating other job applications. While not paying a great deal, this allowed him to continue to support his family in modest fashion.

The new place, at 12 Wright Street, was a two family affair owned by sweet old Mrs. Bridget O'Brien, who lived across the street at number eleven, and had a mellifluous Irish accent. She had been, in her less affluent days, a housekeeper for, as she told my father one day, "Mr. Charles Eliot Norton. A good man, Mr. Burrows, but he was a heathen." The rent was twenty dollars a month for the upper half of the house, which had a finished attic.

The apartment had a living room facing the street, a dining room behind that, then a pantry leading into the kitchen. The kitchen contained, in addition to the oil-cloth covered table, which my father derisively referred to as the catch-all, four wooden chairs, a sink, and a gas stove with burners on top, and an oven beneath. A wire frame could be positioned over one of the burners, which would then be lit with a wooden match from the box holder on the wall next to the stove. Slices of bread would be leaned against the frame to be toasted. These had to be watched closely, as the bread went almost instantly from totally white to pitch black.

It was my job to "watch the toast," a chore I despised almost as much as emptying the icebox water. At a certain point, electric toasters were invented, and my father bought one. These had to be guarded almost as intently, so that the door on either side could be opened and the toast turned around before it burned. Still later a toaster was invented with two slots on the top. "The toast pops up to let you know it's done!" the ad in the Globe proclaimed. I dunned my father until he purchased one, and my life changed wildly for the better. (Years after that, I saw an ad describing yet a further improvement in toasting efficiency. "The toast glides up noiselessly. No annoying pop-up!")

A small hall behind the kitchen housed an icebox, and later on in our tenancy, a refrigerator. In the pre-refrigerator days, the iceman would show up twice a week with a large chunk of ice, which he would carry up the stairs, holding it by giant tongs on a reverse leather apron which protected his back. Comedians told jokes about the fact that when hubby was off at work, the iceman would visit the home: "Every man has his woman, but the iceman has his pick!" The block of ice would be dropped into an insulated compartment at the top of the box. The cold air would then filter down, preserving the food. As the ice melted, the water would drip through passageways on either side of the icebox and collect in a pan on the floor underneath. It would be my job to empty this pan every other day, and pour its contents into the sink. The filled pan was heavy and as I lifted it, invariably the water would slosh back and forth and spill onto the front of my pants. That was not a good look for a boy. When the technology improved and refrigerators were invented (and my father could afford one), the icebox was replaced by a fine Kelvinator, and life got better for the whole family.

To the side of the living and dining rooms was a pair of bedrooms, the smaller one for me and a master bedroom for my parents. In between them was the family bathroom, an unexpectedly large affair, which contained, of all things, a bookcase facing the toilet. As I sat on the commode, I memorized the titles of the books: Thomas Mann's *The Magic Mountain*, *Tramping on Life* by Harry Kemp, *Ten Days That Shook the World* by John Reed and Marx's *Das Kapital*. There was also a copy of Kraft-Ebbing's *Psychopathia Sexualis*, which described in lurid detail human sexual deviances and disturbances. I read it with fascination, but had a problem with the book. Every time the details became really interesting, the text switched to Latin. I bought an English-Latin dictionary at the Harvard Coop, and got a head start on that ancient language because I wanted to know about the man who got into a bathtub filled with oil, accompanied by "tres nudas puellas."

Next to the master bedrooms, there was a screened-in back porch, where I opted to sleep on an old sofa when the weather was clement. The porch also contained an old-fashioned wind-up victrola. I would play 78 rpm records on this, winding the handle and changing the cactus needle after every play. My favorite record was "It's A Long Way to Tipperary," a World War I song.

The apartment had a flight of stairs heading down to the front door, and a second flight going up to the finished attic. There was also a back stairway behind the refrigerator, which led down to a common landing on the ground floor. From there, a flight of steps led to a basement with a furnace and a coal bin. Each year on Ash Wednesday, I would go down to the coal bin and rub my finger on a lump of coal to put a smudge on my forehead, so it would look like I had been to Mass that morning, like all the Catholic boys in the new neighborhood.

It was also in this basement that I stacked and tied into bundles, old copies of the Christian Science Monitor, and other periodicals that George read, waiting for the rag man to come by so I could sell them. His name was M. Hyatt, as the sign on the side of his horse drawn wagon read. He would ride through the neighborhood every month or so, calling out in a thick accent of some kind, "Haragg! Haragg!" and I would run out to stop him and lead him "down cellar," as the phrase went. The rag man would weigh the bundles with a hand-held scale, making sure that I could not see the numbers on it and say each time, "You done good, little boy. Nine cents." I would protest that sometimes there were nearly twice as many papers as there had been the month before, but Mr. Hyatt would only laugh and count the pennies into my hand. Then he would urinate on the coal in the bin, saying, "Don' tell your fadda." The aroma from Mr. Hyatt's urine was even more pungent than that of Mr. Hyatt himself, and the cellar would reek for hours. His business finished, Hyatt would haul his bundles away and not be seen for another month.

I was frequently left alone in those days, when my parents went out in the evening to political meetings or to parties. They thought nothing of this and neither did I. Once, when I was nine, they traveled to a convention in Chicago for five days. They gave me money to buy food, and told me they'd phone from time to time to make sure I was all right. Then they picked up their suitcases and walked to the corner of Hudson Street and Massachusetts Avenue (or Mass Ave, as it was always called). A streetcar stopped there and took them south to Harvard Square, where it went underground. From there, they rode the subway to North Station and caught the train to Chicago.

I had joined the Cub Scouts. A boy could belong to a Cub Scout den without being able to afford a uniform. But in order to be able to march in one of the parades which were held from time to time, it was necessary to wear, if not the entire uniform, at least a cap and neckerchief. When my parents left for Chicago, I pocketed the food money. I calculated what a cap and neckerchief would cost, went to scout headquarters, and bought them. I had enough left over for ten cans of Franco-American spaghetti, my favorite. I figured that I could survive perfectly well on two cans a day and that is what I did. My parents called from Chicago as promised, and I told them I was fine, which I was. When they arrived home, saw the neckerchief and cap and realized what he had done, they were furious. But it was too late to do anything about it, and I marched with the Cub Scouts.

Nobody got an allowance in those days. None of my friends; not Elliott Knight nor Basil Bourque nor Bobby Whoriskey. It was unheard of. A boy was expected to figure out how to earn what he needed. And that is what I did. I raked leaves in the autumn and shoveled snow in the winter. I washed windows for five cents a side. When I had saved up enough to buy a used bicycle with a basket on the handlebars, I rode it to Gebott's Bakery in East Cambridge and bought day-old Creme Friedcakes, a delicious confection. I bought these two for a nickel, then peddled them door to door for five cents each. I sold copies of Look Magazine. Lilacs bloomed in vacant lots around Cambridge. I picked them, arranged them in bunches, and sold them out of my red Radio Flyer wagon on busy Mass Ave for ten cents a bunch.

On Memorial Day, people went to the Mount Auburn Cemetery to lay flowers on their loved ones' graves. It was a long hot climb up the hill to the cemetery entrance. I bought quarts of orange soda at the First National Store for four cents a bottle. I bought stacks of paper cups. I purchased a large chunk of ice, stuck it in a galvanized tub of water, cooled the bottles and hauled the whole thing up the hill in my wagon. I sold cups of the cold soda for a nickel each. I got five cups out of each quart. That was twenty one cents profit per quart, less the cost of the cups and ice. I did so well that on subsequent Memorial Days I hired a kid to pull an extra wagon, and nearly doubled my profits.

My paternal grandmother had been born Annie MacRay, in the city of Dundee, in Scotland. My grandfather, James Burrows, born in 1856, was from Belfast in Northern Ireland and was, according to legend, "so full of it" that his nickname was "the Englishman." The pair met on Ellis Island after both had migrated to America. They were married shortly afterwards, and set up housekeeping in Summerville, Mass. Annie Burrows was religious and remained a Scotch Covenanter for all of her short, star-crossed life. Burrows provided her with little more than a succession of children, all of whom, except for George, died young, one in a fiery automobile crash. One day, he went out to buy a quart of milk, and did not return for three years. Annie kept the family alive by taking in washing and scrubbing floors. She went to church on Sunday mornings and Wednesday evenings, taking young George with her.

I never met my father's parents, who died before I was born, or any other of my paternal relations. George had a distrust of relatives. He had, in fact, a distrust of just about everybody. "Never get to know the neighbors," he admonished me. "They'll only want something from you."

The Christian Science Monitor was delivered to the front stoop every weekday. It occasionally featured, for some reason, articles printed in English, and elsewhere on the same page in French. I taught myself basic elements of that language by going back and forth between the two versions. "Bon jour, Georges," I would say to my father, which always made him laugh. I called him George, never dad or pops or father. My mother, I called Marian. They did not find this offensive, they had inaugurated it. It seemed to them the modern way of doing things.

Politics ran rampant in our house. Fundraisers were held. Committees were formed and disbanded. Harry Bridges, the famous San Francisco organizer of longshoremen, came and spoke to a group of George's activist friends. Two of the

Scottsboro Boys came. They were young southern Black men, who had been falsely accused of rape. Left-wing legal groups had sprung them from jail, and then trotted them around to sympathetic northern households, where glasses of rye and ginger were peddled for fifty cents a shot to raise money "for the cause." I remembered these names because my father had given me an autograph book and told me to have guests sign it. I would have preferred to have had Jack Benny's signature. The comings and goings in the house were little more than a distraction to me.

Endless discussions about "the people" were held in the living room or up in the finished attic. Anarchists debated with socialists and Trotskyites argued with Mensheviks. Guests left their coats and pocket books in my room. No one asked my permission to do this, and since I considered myself one of the people, I thought it only fair that I open a few of the purses on my bed and help myself to a bit of pocket change.

One of the organizations George belonged to was called The League Against War and Fascism. When Josef Stalin made the surprise announcement that he had concluded a non-aggression pact with Adolph Hitler, the name of the organization changed overnight to The League for Peace and Democracy. That was when it began to occur to George that Moscow might be having a say in what went on in his living room.

The consumption of rye and ginger at the fund raisers spilled over into every day life, though in my mother's case, her preference was for wine. Arguments ensued; these turned into fights. She began drinking in private, and hiding the empties. Her housekeeping, never first class, became less so. Annie MacRay Burrows, though church-mouse poor, had kept her flat spotless. George expected no less from his wife. The beautiful Marian, worshipped by the public and celebrated by The Boston Globe, did not tend to live up to his housekeeping standards. He would come home from his job at the W.P.A. and demand to know what she had done all day. She told him it was harder than he knew to keep a place clean.

Once, he concealed a dollar bill under a broom in the hallway beside the fridge. When he got back from work that day, he asked if she had swept the house. "Sure I did," she bristled. Then, with a roar of triumph, he lifted the broom and she saw the dollar bill on the floor beneath it. Bursting into tears, she fled the kitchen and ran into their bedroom. Sorry then, for the mean trick he'd played, he followed to console her, locked the bedroom door behind him, and they wound up making love. I sat at the oil-cloth covered table in the kitchen, listening to the muted sounds of passion, having been sent by Central Casting to play the small but dramatic role of the child.

There were, of course, some happy moments in the house on Wright Street. I loved the Christmas season. My father would select a tree from the corner stand on Mass Ave. It would be set up in the living room and decorated with multi colored lights, garlands and tinsel. I would always beg to be allowed to sleep on the couch in the front room with the tree, and for its lights to be left on until I had fallen asleep. The beauty of it cheered my heart more than anything I could imagine. Christmas carols were sung in school, stores were decorated for the season, and people on the street greeted one another with, "Merry Christmas." But Christmas time couldn't last forever and bad things were to come.

III

My mother's warnings about doing harm to herself intensified, and became darker and more frequent.

"I may have to go far, far away."

"Can't I go with you?"

"No, this is someplace I have to go alone."

"But why?"

"Just because, that's all."

It always finished that way, leaving me anxious and worried. I increased the wooing of my father, feigning interest in his work, and asking to visit him at the office. Flattered by the attention, he began taking me on what he called meanders, long rambling walks around the neighborhood, during which he lectured me on matters arcane and sometimes occult. There were stories about events in the distant past, and seminars on the history of America and the thirteen original colonies. These were genuinely interesting, and I realized that he was doing the best he could to play the role of parent. The meanders did not include my mother, and she resented them, which only seemed to add to my father's pleasure.

One tension-filled Friday evening, an argument more vociferous than usual erupted. My mother was convinced that George was seeing a woman on the side. Her name, as I gathered from overheard conversations was Rosebud. He was steadfast in his denials. On the evening in question, as a sort of sour joke, Marian presented him with a half-pint of Four Roses whiskey. He smashed the bottle in the sink and stormed into the bedroom. She followed and closed the door behind her. The din of the argument gradually abated and was replaced by the muted sound of pleasure. I sat at the oil-cloth covered table for a while, then got up and went to the sink to retrieve the shards of broken glass from the whiskey bottle.

The following morning, my mother, unable to leave well enough alone, brought the subject up again. My father responded with fury.

"Rosebud, Rosebud! Can't you talk about anything but Rosebud?"

"I'm sure you don't mind talking about her when you're over there with her!"

"Well, If I do, it's not about what a lousy job she does keeping the house clean!"

"So you admit that's where you go all these nights when you're not home!"

"Oh, for God's sake! Come on, Dallas. Let's get the hell out of here." He stormed down the front stairs and out the door. I followed, anxious as always, to ensure that he should ultimately return. As we strode away, my mother leaned out of the upstairs window.

"I'll be dead when you get back!" she screamed. "You'll find me on the floor in front of the oven!" These prognostications were happening with ever increasing frequency.

"Maybe she means it this time, George." I tried to appear casual but my guts were heaving.

"It's just an act. You'll see." The meander went on for the best part of an hour; I became increasingly anxious. Finally we headed for home.

As we rounded the corner onto Wright Street, George pointed to the curtain in the upstairs window. It seemed to be fluttering slightly.

"See there? That's where she's been waiting, watching for us." I wasn't so sure the curtain had been moving. The window was open a crack; maybe it was a breeze. We entered the front hall, and climbed the stairs. A strong smell of gas permeated the apartment, coming from behind the closed door of the kitchen. I had smelled it before.

"George..." I was really frightened. My father snorted in derision.

"We'll call her bluff. You'll see." Into my parents' room we stormed, closing the door but leaving it unlocked. George opened the bedroom windows to clear the air. Minutes passed, which seemed like hours to me.

"Don't you think we ought to..."

"Naw. I tell you it's a bluff." And sure enough, finally the gas smell abated, the bedroom door opened and my mother stood there, furious and humiliated. I made my escape; later on I heard the sounds of passion.

I often thought about things: is there a God? Are we all just characters in his dreams, and when he wakes up, will we disappear? I was attracted to the idea of re-incarnation. It made sense to me. I figured I must have done some really bad stuff in a past life. It was sort of comforting to me to believe that. George and Marian sent me to different Sunday schools "to try them out", but I knew it was just to get me out of the house so they could make love. What I learned on these Sundays was that Congregationalists throw the best Christmas parties, Episcopalians put on elegant Easter pageants (I got to lead a donkey down the aisle at the fancy church just outside Harvard Square with the bullet holes in it from the American Revolution), and Unitarians are no fun at all.

The earliest thought I could remember consciously thinking was that I would break out one day and be happy. I considered myself sort of a prisoner, perhaps a trustee who could come and go sometimes, but was still locked up. The phrase "break out" came from the Warner Brothers' prison pictures I had started going to, and loved. I was fascinated when death row inmates walked "the last mile." As the condemned man passed a row of cells, an African-American inmate in one of them would play "Goin' Home" on the harmonica, and another con would call out, "See ya later, Johnny."

My favorite death row walker (well everybody's, I supposed) was Jimmy Cagney, pretending to snivel in fear as they dragged him to his death. Pat O'Brien, the good priest, had convinced him that tough kids in Hell's Kitchen (who admired Cagney's bravado) would be dissuaded from a life of crime if they heard that he'd gone to the chair acting cowardly. The movies saved my life, in a way. At home there was no right or wrong; it was all a jumbled-up mess. At the pictures, crime didn't pay, good deeds were rewarded, and dreams came true. Spencer Tracy tried and tried and wouldn't give up, and finally invented the light bulb (and just about everything else). Edward G. Robinson found the "magic bullet" that cured syphilis. Greer Garson discovered radium. Don Ameche came up with the telephone. Paul Muni created pasteurization. I would walk out of the movies, blinking in the late afternoon sun, thinking, "It can be done. I can do it. I will do it."

In the pictures, there was no weird sexual stuff going on. Even married couples slept in separate beds. Life was clean and wholesome. Bing Crosby, a good priest, helped troubled kids in his parish play basketball instead of stealing cars. Edward G. Robinson ended a life of crime by expiring on the steps of a church and crying out, "Mother of God, is this the end of Rico?" Movies did for me what Sunday School failed to do. They gave me a conscience.

I knew the name of every supporting player in films. Jack Norton played a comic drunk. Grady Sutton and Franklin Pangborn were W. C. Fields' foils. In the M.G.M. historical dramas, I always looked for Edna May Oliver, Donald Crisp and Dame May Whitty. Edward Arnold was an evil capitalist. (Everyone knew who Henry Fonda was; I could spot Edward Arnold).

Movies replenished my soul. Life at home was so toxic that when I slept in my inside room in winter, I moved the bed against the wall and opened the window. Bundling up with extra covers to keep warm, I laid my pillow on the windowsill and drifted off to sleep with my head literally outside the house, breathing in the cold, clean, fresh night air. Once I glanced at the living room wall and saw germs crawling by the millions. Looking back as an adult, I realized that I had actually had a psychedelic experience.

Learning to expect the unexpected was a necessary survival tool at 12 Wright Street. George came home one day with a tea cart. That was what he called it. It was made of blonde wood, had an upper and lower level, and four rubber-tired wheels. I could not see that it served any purpose at all, but my father was crazy for it. He kept it upstairs in the finished attic, and perhaps planned to serve rye and ginger from it when fund-raisers were held. My boyhood friends, who occasionally came to the house and were attracted to the attic because of its large open space, could see a use for the tea cart. Even though warned repeatedly by me not to "fool with it," they couldn't resist lying on the cart and propelling themselves across the floor. Suddenly in mid-flight, a cracking noise was heard, and one of the lower legs holding a wheel was off and lying on its side.

I was terrified. I sent my friends packing and went downstairs to find my mother. "We've got to find a carpenter and get it fixed," she told me. Conspiring together, we looked in the phone book and made a call. Yes, Mr. Mahoney could do the job if the table were brought to him. I wheeled the injured cart, holding up the corner with the snapped off leg down Mass Ave, through Harvard Square and half way to Kerry Corner, a neighborhood given that name because so many Irishmen from county Kerry lived there. Kindly Mr. Mahoney saw that the table could easily be mended by inserting a dowel, then gluing the leg, and that no-one would ever know that a fracture had taken place. I was vastly relieved, paid for the work and raced the cart home in time for it to be taken to the attic before my father's return. Mother and son agreed that it would be our secret.

A week later, George and Marian were having one of their knock-down, drag-out fights. George retreated to the master bedroom and locked the door. My mother stood outside and wailed. There was a lull in the festivities when she went to the bathroom. I tapped on the bedroom door. My father opened it, let me in and then re-locked it. This infuriated Marian but was part of my plan to convince Pop that he and the kid were buddies (thereby saving Mama's life). My mother banged on the door.

"Dallas, let me in," she cried. George snorted.

"Do you want me to tell your father something?" she called through the door. I froze in fear. "Well, do you," she asked?

George looked over at me. "What's going on?" he said. "Does she have something on you?"

"No." I muttered. But I opened the door. Marian entered triumphantly. I slinked out and went to my room. Another week went by and yet another maelstrom ensued. Screaming, cursing, locking of doors, my being let in, my mother pounding.

Again: "Do you want me to tell your father something?" Sold out by my tea cart ally, I had no choice but to unlock the door. The third time it happened, I realized that blackmail never stops costing. I took a deep breath, looked at my father and said, "A friend of mine broke your tea cart. I had it fixed."

"Oh that," he said. "Yeah. She told me about that back when it happened."

1938 was the year the New York World's Fair opened in Queens. I became obsessed with going to it. I read everything I could find about it in The Christian Science Monitor, and looked at photos of the Trilon and Perisphere in Look Magazine. I begged George to take me to the fair, and to my absolute delight my father agreed to do so. We would travel to New York City by train, George told me, and "take in the sights." But the year came and went, and no trip was forthcoming. The fair was scheduled to re-open for a second year, and once more I was assured that we would attend. As the1939 season drew to a close, I reminded my father again and again of his promise. The fair shut down. I was devastated.

But George had other plans. "You're going to get something way better than a trip to some old fair," he told me. "You, my boy, are going to be 'Millionaire for a Day'!" Asked what that meant, George replied, "It means exactly what it sounds like. A millionaire gets to do anything he wants, right?" I acknowledged that that sounded right to me. "Well," said George, "for one day you get to do anything you want."

"No matter what it costs?"

"A millionaire doesn't have to worry about money."

Elated, I ran from the house to the direction of Bowdoin Street. This was where I hung out with my friends: Elliott, Basil, Bobby and the others. Together, we had formed a group called "The Bowdoin Street Hell Drivers." Using wooden orange crates, attached to lengths of two-by-four, with roller skate wheels screwed under them, we had fashioned home-made scooters, which we raced up and down the block past crabby old Mr. Graustein's weed-filled garden. I found the boys, and told them of my great good fortune.

"I can buy you all anything you want for one day," I crowed. A mighty cheer emerged from the hell drivers, and they picked me up and carried me the length of the block on their shoulders.

I selected a date and told my father. "Alright," said George, "Now you have to make up a budget." I looked questioningly at him.

"Even a millionaire needs a budget," said George. "Tell me what you want to spend. Do you want to take the subway into Boston? That's a nickel. Are you going to bring a friend along? That makes it ten cents. Both going to drink a soda? That's another dime. A movie? There's twenty cents more." As my father spoke, the awful truth dawned on me. It had been one more scam, one more ruse, another lie added to a string of lies. Two years of waiting for the World's Fair, and now this. And I had to tell the hell drivers.

Things went from bad to worse. George would accuse my mother of drinking, and she'd deny it. He'd find his proof in hidden empty wine bottles, and storm out of the house. Marian would race after him and I would wait, hoping they'd return together. But more often than not she came back alone in tears. I would retreat to my room and turn in. Sometimes she'd find me in my bed, sit on the edge of it, rub my back and tell me stories of her girlhood in Vermont. At these moments I wanted to throw my arms around her and say that I loved her best in all the world. Instead I'd lie stiffly, thinking to protect my pride from further hurt. I knew that when George inevitably returned in a night or so, I would revert to my familiar walk-on role in the melodrama, one not even worth being mentioned in the playbill.

One night my parents fought, and he raged out of the house with her fast on his heels. I waited anxiously for more than an hour. The phone rang and I rushed to pick up the receiver. A mans voice asked, "Is this Dallas Burrows?"

"Yes."

"This is Officer Johnson of the Cambridge police department. Do you know where your father is?" I began to tremble, filled with fear.

"He went out with my wife..." I realized I had made an embarrassing slip of the tongue. "I mean my mother."

"Well, I'm afraid something has happened to her..." My heart stopped. There was a pause, and then the sound of muffled hilarity filled the earpiece. I heard the policeman's voice change to that of my father.

"I'm sorry Dallas, it's just a joke," he laughed. "I'm with her. We're at a bar across from Sears Roebuck. You know where it is?" I did.

"Come on and join us. We'll wait for you there." I wiped my eyes, filled with equal parts of fury and relief. I threw on a jacket and raced out the door. Years later, I couldn't remember what the bar had looked like, or what had been said, or how we all walked home together, except that we did.

Marian's secret drinking increased. When George came home from work he would inspect the trashcan for wine bottles. She took to stashing the empties, for some reason, in the clothes closet of my bedroom (I was sleeping out on the back porch). George would discover them and I would be drawn into the sordid drama. A fight would ensue. Sometimes my father would leave; sometimes he'd forgive her and they'd retreat to the bedroom to make love. But always there was drama.

A family acquaintance came to visit one night, a newspaper reporter for whom George had once gotten a job. There were drinks and there was camaraderie. I turned in for the night out on the back porch. I stirred in my sleep at eleven, hearing the sounds of retirement in the master bedroom next to the porch. But when I awakened early the next morning, I realized that something was wrong. I walked down the hall and looked into my bedroom. The friend and my mother were asleep in my bed. Terrified, I moved back past my parents' bedroom and onto the back porch. When I heard my father open his door and head for the bathroom, I stopped him.

"George," I began, and pointed toward my bedroom.

"It's alright, Dallas," my father whispered. "Go back to bed." I did as I was told, and somehow fell asleep again. When I re awakened, the reporter was gone and the incident was never discussed.

IV

Once a year, there came a relief from the purgatory that was Cambridge. This was when my mother and I went to spend summers in Hartland, Vermont. We had made the trip for as far back as I could remember. My father had gone with us once. It had not been a fortuitous experience, so since that time we had vacationed without him. This meant that George spent summers home alone in Cambridge. He would accompany us to North Station and put us on the train to White River Junction. There, my grandfather would pick us up in his Buick, a car he had nick-named The Super-Dreadnaught. It had, when he had originally bought it, been one of the first automobile to be driven in and around Hartland, and had been an object of widespread revulsion among the local farmers. (Years later I sat with him on his ninety-fourth birthday, and watched Neil Armstrong take his first steps on the moon. It was then that Grandpa Pollard had shared his memory of being screamed at to "get that thing off the road!" I had marveled at the time span in the room, which went from horseless carriage to moon walk.)

Grandfather and grandmother Pollard's summer place in Hartland was sunny and open. The main room of the house was a large and comfortable space, dominated by the elder Dallas' roll top desk, a horse-hair sofa and a Franklin stove. A dining room table stood in the middle of the room, but was never used for eating. Instead, it supported a Tiffany lamp, the cord to which hung from an overhead light fixture. A small side table with a Philco radio on it, stood next to the desk. In front of that was a rocking chair, where Katherine, a devoted fan of the Red Sox, would sit and listen to the intermittently audible game broadcasts from Boston.

The kitchen was dominated by a big wood-burning stove. A sink stood on the opposite wall. It contained a drain, but no connection to running water, which had to be carried in from the pump outside the back door. When I was old enough, it became my job to prime the pump with a bucket of water, which sat on a little wooden platform next to it. After several of my summers in Hartland, running water was installed in the sink, and a bathroom replaced the out-house next to the wood shed.

Behind the shed was a two-story barn which, to me, was a wonderland. It had horse stalls in back, and a hayloft up above. If you went around the side of the barn and down behind it (passing dozens of blackberry bushes, the fruit of which produced thrillingly delicious pies), there were two more horse stalls under the ground floor, one of which housed a winter sleigh with runners. The aroma of the whole barn was magical: a mélange of horses and horse buns and hay.

My grandmother, Katherine, was a rather exacting woman, not unlike her husband's own mother, Sarah (Calvin Coolidge's aunt). I met great-grandmother Sarah Pollard only once, when we were all invited to Sunday dinner (at noon) in her house at Proctorsville. The old lady sat at the head of the table, said salt when she needed it, and that was about all. Later on that Sunday afternoon, she found me, her five year old great-grandson, playing with a slingshot, took it away and kept it.

Katherine's mother, Hattie, on the other hand was a woman with the sweetest of dispositions. She lived with the Pollards in Burlington in the winter, and Hartland in the summer. Hattie, in her nineties, loved her great-grandson, and would pack picnic sandwiches for the two of us. Together, we would climb the steep hill behind the houses across the way from grandpa Pollard's place, spread our blanket and enjoy lunch together. When I was just learning to read, I would sound out the Sunday funnies as my great-grandmother listened patiently. "Donnervetter!" and "Himmel!" from the Katzenjammer Kids were my favorite words to sound out.

Grandpa Pollard adored his daughter, and grew to love me as well. But he disapproved of her choice of a husband. George was a New Deal Democrat before the term existed. Marian's younger brother Gene, a dental surgeon in Boston, and his wife Elizabeth, would join his sister and me at the Pollards' summer house for a week or two each summer. His view of George Burrows was even dimmer than that of his parents. I came to love my grandfather deeply. His strong character ("Whatever is worth doing, is worth doing well.") influenced me in ways I came to understand and admire as I grew into adulthood.

The Pollard's house was the last in a line of forty or so houses that began in the town square of Hartland Three Corners (there was a Hartland Four Corners but the family rarely visited it), and headed north. Hartland Three Corners, or Hartland as everybody called it, boasted a First National Store, an independent market, a post office, a barber shop and a sizeable brick meeting place called Damon Hall, where occasional Country and Western concerts were held and 4 H Club gatherings took place. A small triangular patch of grass stood in the center of the town, if it could be called a town. The triangle contained the statue of a Civil War veteran.

In the third house up the road, a little way past the First National Store, lived a weather-beaten old character named Lon Merritt. Grandmother Katherine disapproved of him ("a loafer and nothing else"), but at the age of five, I found him fascinating. Happy to have a willing ear, Lon would share his experiences in the French Foreign Legion, and his years in the British Navy ("The old fool has never been farther from home than Rutland!").

One day, I sat beside him on a bench in his back yard, as he prepared his dinner. He had purchased a bag of onions at the First National, and was getting ready to sauté them in a fine old iron spider, over the charcoal fire he'd lit on his grill. My eyes watered as I watched the old man slice the onions. Then, I realized to my absolute astonishment that the onion slices were coming out in perfect concentric rings. I had never seen anything like it in my life. With wide (watery) eyes, I asked him how on earth he had learned to do such a thing. He glanced around as if to make sure that no-one was listening, then explained the mystery. "An Egyptian pharaoh," he said, "died in my arms. I'd saved his life years before, you see, and he was forever grateful. So with his last breath, wanting to give me something valuable, you understand, he whispered out the secret of how to slice onion in rings." Excited as hell, and anxious to share the news, I ran at top speed to my grandparents' home. I was sure that this information would vindicate my belief in the old man's value.

"Oh that fool," my grandmother snapped. "That worthless old fool. Now get out of here and find yourself something helpful to do for your grandfather."

At the end of the line of houses on the Woodstock road, beyond the Pollard's place, was a sort of mini-canyon, in which the elder Dallas' garden grew, and through which Lull Brook flowed. The garden produced, among other things, corn, beets, string beans, lettuce, asparagus and tomatoes. When corn was in season, grandpa would position a big galvanized pot on the wood-burning stove. The water having begun to boil, he would pull out his pocket watch, in what became a ritual. "Corn isn't worth eating," he would say, "if it's not in the water within five minutes of being picked."

I would dash out of the kitchen through the screened-in back porch, and down the hill to the garden. Rapidly selecting a dozen ears of the succulent yellow corn, I would rush back up the hill and into the house. "Two minutes," grandpa would announce, holding up his fine old railroad watch. Shucking the corn at mach ten speed, I would drop the ears into the churning water just as he shouted, "Time!" The corn was so fresh and delicious that it hardly needed butter and salt. Sometimes, when it was in season, dinner consisted of nothing but heaps of corn, eaten with butter and salt anyway, and completely mouth watering. Then, when corn season was over, we waited for another year;

no produce shipments from Mexico in those days. Asparagus season lasted only two weeks. The family ate asparagus on toast, sometimes twice a day, and cream of asparagus soup. Then, as with the corn, there was another year's wait.

On August first, grandfather Pollard would hand me a quarter to run down to the general store for Hire's root beer extract. Together, we would mix the extract with sugar and water, boil it up, and "can" it in two dozen Ball jars. These would then be stored down in the cool damp basement under the house for the several weeks needed for the root beer to ferment. For me, the wait was an agony. Meanwhile, other items were being preserved. Beets, string beans, rhubarb, corn, all of these, as their time came, were cooked, took their place in Ball jars, and were sealed with rubber rings for dining in the winter to come. Down in the basement, an occasional explosion would be heard as a jar of root beer "popped." When the beverage was finally ready, I found the taste delicious beyond description.

Beyond the valley containing Grandpa Pollard's garden and the little burbling brook, the ground rose again. On this spot, mercifully hidden from Grandmother Pollards view by a row of trees, sat the home of the Howe family. The structure had originally been little more than a tar-paper shack, and its inhabitants had been, as the phrase went in those days, on relief. This meant that the family, dirt poor, had practically nothing. The state of Vermont wasn't actually going to let them die, so the shack, doubtless seized from somebody else for non-payment of taxes, had been given to the Howes.

But that family, defying expectations, did not just squat in the hovel they'd received. They were a large clan, with a number of strapping sons, and they set about turning their new home into something quite livable. Rooms were added, linoleum was laid and, there apparently being no building code supervisors interested in interfering, the work was done in record time.

The youngest of the Howe children, a boy named Avery, who was my age, became my summer friend when both of us were ten. To a casual observer, the Howe family might have looked like the Beans of Egypt, Maine. But I saw through the externals and found a joyousness that overwhelmingly attracted me. At breakfast time, all eight or ten of the clan would sit down at the round table in the kitchen. Mrs. Howe would have prepared an extra-large pot of Rockwell's Cocoa, using the cocoa powder, plenty of sugar and water. A loaf of First National Brand bread would sit on the table, still in its wrapper, while next to it rested a slab of uncolored oleomargarine.

In those days, as I well knew from back home in Cambridge, margarine had no buttery tint, but was white and resembled lard. A small envelope containing bright orange powder, similar to that which comes today in packages of Kraft Macaroni and Cheese, accompanied the slab. In order to make the spread take on at least a semblance of the hue of butter, it was necessary to place it in a bowl, sprinkle the powder on it and then knead it at great length, until it achieved the desired color. This was my job at 12 Wright Street, another chore which I despised. When I asked my father why the company couldn't just sell the margarine with the color of butter in the first place, George would deliver a diatribe on the near-criminal monopoly of the dairy industry.

The Howes just didn't bother. They slathered the lard-colored oleo onto the soft white bread, dipped it into the communal cauldron of cocoa, and chomped away. They filled their tin cups from the pot, and slaked their thirst. On the mornings I was invited to join them, I thought I had never tasted a finer breakfast in all my life. The table was filled with love and laughter, and if I had been asked to become a member of the family, I would have accepted the invitation in an instant. Grandmother Katherine was deeply offended. "Why do you go over there to that dreadful house, where they have nothing, and eat that terrible stuff, when you can sit down right here and have eggs?"

It seemed like everyone in the Howe family made music. Mrs. Howe played the tinny upright piano in the living room, and all the boys had guitars. "Turn your radio on and listen to the Savior. Tune in over station S-A-V-E-D," they crooned. And "Old dog Tray ever faithful. Grief will not drive him away" Every evening was concert time, chez Howe, and I was there as often as I could get away. The family enchanted me. Avery and I rode our bicycles up and down Main Street, and looked for money-making odd jobs together. Avery seemed to worship the skinny city boy from Boston, and would do anything I asked of him.

Once a summer, I put on a show in Hartland. My grandparents had given me, for my birthday, a Gilbert Magic Set. There were cups and balls, linking rings, Chinese Sticks, and instructions for many other tricks to be performed with cards, thimbles and cigarettes to be filched from my mother's pack of Kools. I had practiced these industriously in my room in Cambridge and developed, over time, a serviceable magic act. The shows I produced in Hartland were really just an excuse to perform these tricks, but I surrounded them with additional acts and events, and these usually starred my friend. One year, Avery and I sank two iron poles into the ground at the base of the hill behind the Howe house. The poles were set four feet apart. We spread layers of brown paper between them, and soaked the paper with kerosene.

At the top of the hill, we constructed a ramp, on top of which sat Avery's bicycle. At the end of my magic act, with twenty or twenty five neighbors and the Howe family making up the audience, I announced that Mr. Avery Howe, the renowned thrill rider, would propel his bike through the fiery wall of death! As Avery's mother watched with apprehension, I ran down the hill, lit the kerosene soaked paper with my grandfather's cigar lighter, and gave the signal. Avery pushed off from the ramp and raced down toward the now blazing barrier. As his mother let out a shriek, her son crashed through the flames, and the crowd roared its approval.

"That's it, never again!" cried Mrs. Howe. But the following summer, Avery starred once more. That year, the show was put on in the entryway to my grandparent's barn, with benches and chairs set up outside on the dirt driveway for the spectators. On the front of the barn, at the second story level, was a wide door, which led to the hayloft. In the days when wagonloads of hay would be delivered, this door would be opened and the hay, stacked high, would be pitch-forked into the upper level loft. On the front of this door, I had attached a sign on which I had printed in bold black letters: WATCH THIS DOOR FOR THE BIG SURPRISE! Underneath the sign I performed my magic.

In the carriage house, as an added attraction, there was a side show featuring neighborhood kids who appeared as bearded lady, thin man, world's tallest midget, world's shortest giant, etc. In front of the barn, when I had finished my last trick and the audience had applauded, I drew their kind attention to the hayloft door a flight and a half above, and introduced "the great parachute jump." That door now opened and Avery Howe appeared, holding above him an old carriage umbrella. Six feet across, it was constructed of a heavy canvas-like material, with metal spokes and fringe. In all probability, it weighed more than Avery himself. We had found it in the dark recesses of the lower barn.

As his mother once again stood to scream in protest, Avery leapt from the loft door and plummeted like an anvil to the ground below. Several men rushed to the carriage umbrella, which was all that anyone could see, lifted it up and saw Avery grinning up at them from the driveway. Grandmother Pollard graciously consented to speak with Mrs.Howe and it was agreed that Avery would appear in no more of her grandson's productions.

Hartland's main claim to fame was its annual fair. This took place on the fair grounds, a fifteen minute walk from the center of town. A three-day event, held around Labor Day, it was a sizeable affair, and drew people from across the southern part of the state. There were sulky races and oxen pulls, in which the animals competed with each other, hauling huge slabs of granite. There were long barracks, empty all year, which housed for three days, prize geraniums, prize cattle, prize roosters, prize hogs and prize anything that I could imagine. Pies were baked, tasted and acclaimed. Home-made quilts were displayed and marveled over. Country bands performed on the grandstand. There were rides of all kinds, and a Ferris wheel. There were hot dogs and hamburgers, and there was cotton candy. There was a tent that housed a show called Secrets of Chinatown, which promised that the farmers who forked over (the sizeable amount of) 25 cents to enter, would see a "Live Naked Girl!"

And there were the gambling booths. Working at odd jobs over the summer, I had saved up the considerable sum of ten dollars, all of it ear-marked for spending at the fair. I was, needless to say, among the earliest arrivals on the Saturday morning, when the gates to the fairgrounds opened. One of the first attractions I came to on the midway was an open tent which housed a large horizontal roulette wheel. When the carnie in charge set the wheel spinning, a live mouse was released from the center of the wheel. The poor thing ran this way and that, desperately looking for a haven of safety. Around the outside rim of the wheel, were brightly colored cups: red, blue and yellow. Bets could be placed on corresponding squares of color where "marks" like me stood. If the mouse scampered into a red cup, the bet placed on red was doubled. I stood watching in fascination. There seemed to be no way the game could be rigged, and it looked like a heaven-sent opportunity to double my money.

Within half an hour, the ten dollars was gone. I was in shock. I wandered the fair grounds, looking at but not riding the Tilt-a-Whirl, and smelling but not tasting the hot dogs. I did manage, on the fair's second day, together with Avery, to find a way to crawl under a loose flap in the back of the tent that housed "Secrets of Chinatown" and watch the show for free. The production lasted fewer than five minutes. An "actor" in dreadful yellow make-up, looking less Oriental than grandfather Pollard, portrayed the villain of the piece. The tragic plot concerned a naïve young woman who, though warned by her family of the dangers of visiting Chinatown, could not resist doing so and was captured and sold to an evil Mandarin.

"Ahhh, my heart of Jade," gloated the Mandarin. "Let us see what beauty lies hidden beneath your clothing!" With that, he ripped off the girl's dress. She screamed, posed nude for an instant, and then swooned. Black-out!... and the Mandarin, dropping his terrible accent, announced, "Alright, boys. For an additional thin dime you can move into the annex, and see what you really came to see." Grumbling, the majority of the rubes shuffled out of the tent.

My earliest Vermont memory took place on a hot summer afternoon in Windsor, the next town over from Hartland, and a much bigger one. The year was 1930 and I was two. Or maybe it was 1931 and I was three. How far back does memory go? When it comes to humiliation, perhaps the answer is pre-natal. The event happened in the back yard of Gerald and Ruth Cabot (no relation to the Cabots and the Lodges). They were fast friends of the Pollard's. The Cabots had some dough, and lived in a fine big house on Main Street, Windsor's main thoroughfare, lined on both sides with elm trees. On the afternoon in question, they were throwing a back-yard barbecue for a sizeable crowd. The guests included Katherine and Dallas Pollard, their daughter Marian, her brother Gene and his wife, and, of course, me.

There was, no doubt, corn on the cob and lots to drink; I don't remember, having been only two or three. What I do remember is that after a long afternoon of playing with other young children in attendance, I was tired. I had been wearing a sun suit. My mother removed it, and Gerald sprayed me with a garden hose, to my delight. I then lay down, naked and innocent on a fringed lap robe from grandpa Pollard's Buick, and took a late afternoon nap.

The grown-ups continued to celebrate until the sun began to set. The Pollards were ready to leave, and Uncle Gene volunteered to pick me up. Which is what he did, literally. He took hold of me, fast asleep, by the arm and pulled me up off the lap robe…which came up with me. Somehow, as I had dozed off in the hot afternoon sun, I had tied two pieces of the blanket's fringe in a knot around my poor little member.

"Look. It's stuck to his *thing!*" a woman shrieked, and the guests howled with laughter (how could they not). Uncle Gene managed to undo the fringe, wrap me in the lap robe, and bundle me into the car. The family contained its mirth until they reached home, and I had been tucked in for the night. But later, as I was drifting off to sleep, I heard the sounds of hilarity echoing through the house.

———•———

I could not help but notice how much happier and livelier my mother seemed, when away from George, and in the bosom of her natal family. But as Labor Day approached each year, she always became anxious to get back to Cambridge and her husband. And I knew that when that happened my high wire act would begin again.

V

It was a Sunday afternoon in early December. I was thirteen, and the year was 1941. George had given me money to go to the local Brigham's, one of a chain of high-end ice cream parlors scattered through the Boston area. Brigham's sold a delicious hot fudge sundae for fifteen cents, and it could be purchased "to go." They offered a smaller version for a dime. So, as the ritual had evolved, George would give me twenty cents on Sunday afternoons, and I would run to the nearest Brigham's, buy two of the smaller sundaes, rush home with them, and my father and I would eat them in the master bedroom. This had become one of a number of rituals which more and more frequently excluded my mother.

Marian had originally set up a tense sort of triangle involving father, mother and son, by enticing me to woo her husband and keep him at home. My father had stayed home, and at first I was odd man out in the arrangement, when they would shut me out of the room. Gradually, the balance had shifted, and now Marian was on the outs. I didn't understand it then, and I barely understand it now. I hadn't set it in motion but, like a good trooper, I played the part in which I'd been cast, as the soap opera continued to evolve. On the Sunday afternoon in question, I had raced home faster then usual. I had news to tell my father, which I'd heard from the counter people at Brigham's.

"Turn the radio on," I cried, out of breath as I arrived. "The Japanese have bombed Pearl Harbor. The country's at war!" The next day, George stayed home from work and the family gathered around the big Philco in the living room and heard the president speak of the dagger that had been thrust into the soft underbelly of the nation. Quickly, life changed at twelve Wright Street, and in America. George's job at the WPA was no longer needed, and he secured an executive position at a shipyard in Boston harbor. That facility was suddenly operating around the clock, with the nation desperate to rebuild the navy the Japanese had sunk in Hawaii. George's job was to see to it that the right people were in the right position, and were doing what they were supposed to do. He was intermittently successful. Because he was forty two years old, he avoided selective service. Marian's younger brother Gene, even though he had two children under the age of five, was drafted because the navy needed dental surgeons to operate on jaw and mouth wounds in the South Pacific.

I supported the war effort in any way I could. I saved tin foil and poured grease drippings from the frying pan into jam jars. Both the foil and the grease were used, I was told, in the making of ammunition. I bought savings stamps to help finance the war. When not in school, I kept the radio on to hear the news. Within a week, Tin Pan Alley had cranked out the first World War II song: "You're a Sap, Mr. Jap (to make Uncle Sammy angry)."

Food rationing was instituted, and books of coupons were distributed. Now that George was making money at the shipyard and the family could afford beef, it was suddenly unpatriotic to eat more than a quarter pound of it (per person) a week. Hamburger at the First National Store on Mass Ave cost nineteen cents a pound, for the better quality, and seventeen cents a pound for the lesser. Marian would give me a nickel to "go buy a quarter pound of ground beef and make sure you tell the butcher to give you the nineteen cent stuff, not the seventeen." Both nineteen and seventeen cent hamburger, when purchased in the amount of a quarter of a pound, cost a nickel. It embarrassed me to make this request.

I began to frequent a store called Holden's Magic Shop. It was located on the twelfth floor of an office building on Tremont Street in Boston. There was a tradition in Holden's that on Saturdays, the best of the local amateur magicians, as well as the occasional pro who happened to be working in town, would gather to hobnob and exchange tricks. Boys (I never saw a girl magician in those days) who were serious about learning magic, were allowed to hang out, observe and learn from their elders. No boy was more serious than I, and I watched and learned how to palm a coin, force a card and do the double lift.

With the pocket money I'd saved from my entrepreneurial endeavors, I was able to purchase equipment at Holden's, like the "change bag," which I could use in a routine called the cut-and-restored necktie, and the card-in-the-balloon effect. My magic act improved greatly and I began to earn money by performing at social functions like the Methodist Church Friday night supper. Two dollars here and two dollars there added up. I also volunteered to entertain at the veterans' hospital where, more than twenty years after the end of the First World War, doughboy victims of gas attacks still sat in wheel chairs staring vacantly at walls.

At the magic shop, a boy my age worked behind the counter on Saturdays and sometimes after school. His name was Parker Swan and he became the idol of all the boys who frequented Holden's. He also became my best friend. We taught each other tricks, went to the pictures together, and ultimately joined the army on the same day. Our friendship lasted for a lifetime.

As the war went on, when Parker and I met for a movie, and then a bite at a Hayes-Bickford cafeteria, all that the restaurant offered for sale was eggs. Everything else, it seemed, was reserved for the troops. I always ordered my eggs poached on toast because, when the yolks broke and saturated the toast, it seemed to me to be more of a meal. "First Cup of Coffee Five Cents," the sign above the counter read. "Second Cup Twenty Five Dollars."

World War II was largely financed by contributions from the country's citizens. People bought War Bonds, thereby loaning the government money, to be paid back with modest interest in ten years (provided America won the war, that is, a prospect which for quite a while seemed less than likely). Hollywood's biggest stars toured in shows which raised money for the war effort. Parker and I attended these at the Boston Garden where, for a quarter, we sat in the upper reaches of the top balcony. Heavy hitters paid hundreds of dollars to sit down front and watch Bob Hope and Bing Crosby sing and clown together, along with the glamorous Dorothy Lamour. I read later that Ms. Lamour had been personally responsible for selling over a hundred and fifty million dollars worth of war bonds!

———•—•———

Perhaps yearning for some uncomplicated love in my life, I began dreaming about owning a dog. I ran the idea past George, who refused, at first, even to consider it. I begged and kept at it, and eventually wore him down. It was agreed that if I got all my homework done on a Friday afternoon, I could take the subway on the following day to Boston, where the city operated a dog pound, and pick one out ("a small one, mind you, that won't eat much.")

I caught the streetcar on Mass Ave and rode it to the underground station in Harvard Square. Then I transferred to the subway, and took that to the Boston Common station, then yet another underground streetcar, for one stop to Tremont Street. I walked from there to the pound, a distance of several blocks. When I arrived at the building, a brick structure with an all-purpose municipal look on Warrenton Street, I took a deep breath, and pushed open the door. I was afraid that at my age, the people in charge would not let me adopt a dog. (I was wrong, as it turned out; they would have let me take every mutt in the place.)

There was a long hallway just inside the front entrance, with double-stacked cages on both sides. Dogs were yapping. More cages were in the inner room. I spoke to the man who appeared to be in charge. There would be a license fee, and that would be that. I began to check out the cages. The number of would-be adoptees was heartbreaking; there were enough dogs to feed half of China. Down the line I walked. In the last cage on the left, I found him: a two-thirds grown part-Shepherd. I touched the cage and the dog licked my fingers through the wire mesh. The love was instantaneous and mutual.

He was too big; I knew that's what George would say. "We can't keep an animal that size. He'll eat us out of house and home." But I had to have him. I signed the form, and handed over the fee: $1.75. I hadn't thought about a leash, but one of the attendants found a length of clothesline. Then he opened the cage and the dog came out and licked my hand again. My heart sang. The attendant tied the rope around the mutt's neck and we were out the door. On the subway, people looked at me and my dog, and smiled. When we arrived at Harvard Square, I decided that instead of taking the streetcar the rest of the way, I would walk Homer home. That was the name I had chosen for my dog. George had made me read The Odyssey.

Homer stopped to sniff at every hydrant, phone pole and bush. When passing cars honked, the dog would start and shiver. I could see that he was skittish. Small wonder, I thought; who knew what he'd been through to wind up in that cage. Well never again, I told myself. Homer was mine now, and he'd always be protected.

When I reached home with my dog, I opened the door to the entryway, then unlocked the inner door. Homer hesitated to enter unknown territory, but I petted and reassured him. We climbed the stairs together. I could hear my father in the kitchen, explaining something to my mother "for the umpteenth time." I led Homer through the living room and the pantry. George stopped in mid-sentence, and took one look at his son and the creature he'd had the temerity to bring home.

"You call that a small dog? No way is that thing staying in this house. Get it out of here!"

"Now, George..." A rare burst of motherliness from Marian. "It's not going to cost us that much." The drama went on for ten minutes, ending with an order for me to "keep it out of the living room and don't let it bite anyone."

I was happy, perhaps really happy for the first time in my life. But I was frightened, too; now I had something to lose. Keeping Homer out of my parents' sight became my preoccupation.

It was late September, Indian-summer of '42. I had bought a proper collar and leash for Homer, who also sported a red bandana around his neck (what the well-dressed dog will wear). We wandered the streets of Cambridge together, pausing at a vacant lot on Linnean Street, where a group of boys, some of whom I knew, were dropping lit firecrackers into ant hills. Homer began to whimper and shake at the noise. I moved on with him, reassuring my dog with soothing tones.

At night, Homer slept at the foot of the cot on the porch, occasionally shivering in his sleep, and waking when a night bird flew past the screen. We gazed into each others' eyes for what seemed like hours on end. Homer would lay his head on his master's lap, glancing up at my face from time to time as if to make sure I was still there.

There came an afternoon when Marian was perched at the oil-cloth table in the kitchen, smoking one of her Kools and nursing a glass of sherry. Unaware of my mother's presence, I walked in with Homer, looking for dog biscuits. When I saw her, I tried to back out, but it was too late.

"C'mere, doggie," she slurred, reaching out her hand.

"Leave him alone," I said. I knew that Homer was nervous around her.

"Don't tell me what to do," my mother said. "C'mere, mutt." She reached out and grabbed the dog's leash. She pulled his muzzle close to her face, and slobbered a boozy kiss on him. The poor thing whimpered and tried to pull away.

"Please leave him alone, Marian. He doesn't like it."

"You respect your mother, damn you. C'mere, dog." She pulled him to her. He tried to back off. She wrestled him closer. He whined, he barked, and then, to my horror, he nipped her cheek.

"Ow!" she shrieked. "Ow, ow!" She let the dog go and it ran to its master.

"I told you, Marian. I told you he didn't like it." Tears were rolling down my face.

"Get out! Get out! You and that damn dog! He bit me!" I took hold of my dog's leash, ran to the porch and closed the door. I was in absolute terror. I sat down on my bed. Homer jumped up onto my lap and we huddled together. Finally, my father came home from work. I heard whispered conversations, my mother tearful. That evening at dinner, nothing was said. I was terrified to bring the matter up, for fear of what I might hear.

For four days, there was no mention of the incident, and I began to convince myself that it might all blow over. I kept the dog out of the house as much as possible. The fourth day was Saturday, and George was home from work. I was on the porch with Homer, playing records on the Victoria, when I heard my father's voice calling to me from the kitchen.

"Come in here, Dallas. I have something for you." I did as I was told.

"Here," said George. "Here's a nickel. Go down to the drugstore and drink a Pepsi there." I was immediately on alert; George had never given me a nickel in my life.

"That's OK," I said. "I don't want a Pepsi". My father scowled.

"Do what I tell you. Take this nickel and go down to the corner."

"I'll go get Homer."

"No, leave him here. Take the nickel." I was terrified. I took the nickel and ran faster than I'd ever run to the drugstore, three blocks away. I swilled the drink and sped home. As I turned the corner of Hudson and Wright, I saw a truck with the words Animal Control printed on it. The truck was pulling away from in front of the house. There was a wire mesh window in the rear door and I could see my dog's face through it.

"Homer!" I screamed, and desperately raced up the block, too late of course. I flew into the house and found my parents in the kitchen.

"Why," I yelled. "Why?"

"It was just a matter of time till he bit someone and we got sued," said George. "If you weren't so selfish, you'd have known that." I stood staring at my parents. Then I stormed onto my room on the porch, slammed the door and sobbed. I sobbed and sobbed and sobbed. I felt as if my heart would break into a million pieces. When there were no tears left, my chest heaved up and down for a long time. Then, I promised myself that they'd never make me cry again.

VI

I had been enrolled in public school in the autumn of my sixth year. The family was living in Fresh Pond. There was no kindergarten in those days; kids started cold turkey in first grade. No blocks and sand, just learning how to read, write and count. The school was a twenty minute hike from home, which I negotiated alone with no problem. My mother would pack me two peanut butter and jelly sandwiches, which she sliced in half and wrapped in wax paper. I carried this lunch to school in a paper bag. A kid on the playground, where the children ate, noticed the contents of my lunch bag one day, and began chanting at me, calling me "Four Sandwich Dallas." I didn't know whether or not to take offense at this and finally decided not to, whereupon the kid, having better things to do, stopped his heckling.

My memories of first grade are dim, except for the day the entire school was taken to my own neighborhood, Fresh Pond, to see the great German zeppelin, the Hindenburg, pass overhead. Hitler had sent it on a promotional tour of American cities. When it appeared in the heavens, it seemed to me the biggest thing I had ever seen, virtually blotting out the sky. It took minutes to pass, and then we all returned to school.

In second grade, when the teacher was momentarily out of the room, I climbed up onto the seat attached to my desk, and began to deliver a talk on some subject or other to the class. This elicited the hoped-for mirth from the children. Unfortunately for me, the teacher returned before my speech had concluded.

"You like it up there? Stay there," she said. My mother was sent for and came to the class room half an hour later, in time to see me still standing on my chair, with tears now streaming down my cheeks. It was clear even to me, that I already had an abnormal need for attention.

Scholastic life was not much better when, half way through third grade the family moved to Wright Street. The Peabody School was a ten minute walk from our new home. Paper turkeys adorned the windows on Thanksgiving, Christmas Carols were sung in December, and my home room teacher, Miss Caine, seemed strict-but-fair. The music instructor had each child audition, before assigning them singing parts in the infrequent concerts. She decided, on hearing my voice, that I should consider myself "a listener" and sit quietly when music was performed. I remembered this years later, when I was belting out show tunes in Broadway musicals.

I finished my primary education at Peabody, having been taught to read, write and count, for which I remain eternally grateful. I also learned, in a course called Civics, that in those days, the American ambassador to Mexico was named George R. Messersmith. I have been unable to forget this fact, and have waited in vain for it to prove to be of some use. There was a ceremony at school when the eighth grade graduated. I was the second smartest boy in the class. The smartest *kid* in the class was a boy named Marshall Goldberg. His name appeared first in the printed ceremonial program. It was followed, in order of accomplishment, by the names of seventeen girls, after which my name appeared, heading the list of remaining twelve students, all boys.

———•◦•———

After graduating from Peabody, I moved on to the Cambridge High and Latin School. I walked half an hour from Wright Street to get there, the last ten minutes of it through Harvard yard. In order to graduate from C.H.L.S., it was necessary to have successfully completed a year of Latin. Despite my research in Kraft-Ebbing, I failed first year Latin, having found the class unbearably boring. In my summer break before sophomore year, I studied at home, and was able to take the make-up test, which was offered in early September. A few days later, the principal of the school called me into his office.

"We're not supposed to tell you this, but I can't resist," he said. "You passed the make-up test with the highest grade in the hundred year history of the school." I then went on to fail second year Latin.

———•◦•———

I basically felt that the only way I could survive high school was to drive the teachers crazier than I felt they were trying to drive me. There was, in the first floor corridor of the school, a statue of Diana. It depicted the goddess reaching back to retrieve an arrow from the quiver strapped to her comely marble shoulder. When I could manage to arrive at school early enough so as not to be seen, I would climb up onto the base on which Diana stood, and string chewing gum between her mouth and the hand that was reaching back for the arrow. It was, in my opinion, an impressive comic effect, and one which drove the teachers crazy.

There was a math instructor, her name long forgotten, who hated the sound of pencils being sharpened. It was, to her, like scratching on glass. The sharpener was attached to a windowsill near her desk. When I came to understand this frailty in my teacher, I orchestrated a posse of like-minded boys to participate in a plot, so that someone was nearly always using the pencil sharpener, and the annoying sound never stopped. These boys were choreographed to arrive from different parts of the classroom, so that a pattern was difficult to discern. The teacher knew that somebody had organized it, but pencils do break, and she was never able to do anything about it other than go quietly mad.

VII

Things went downhill rapidly at twelve Wright Street. Marian's drinking intensified, and she began patronizing a neighborhood bar called, inappropriately, the Elite. It was located on Mass Ave, near the streetcar stop. Sometimes she would get home from an afternoon at the Elite after my father had returned from work, and war would rage in the house.

Outside, war was raging too, and with so many men away from home, lots of jobs became available to industrious boys. There was a luxury hotel in Cambridge called The Continental. When movie stars appeared at the Cambridge Summer Theater, that's where they stayed. I applied for and got a job as busboy in the Continental's dining room. It had white table cloths, candles, and "cuisine." At the Hayes-Bickford, it was "eggs only." The Continental seemed to have no shortage of broiled live lobster. ("Well," I told myself, "I guess you can't ship those overseas to the troops anyway.")

After the summer of '44, I stopped going to Hartland with my mother. I knew that this would hurt my grandfather's feelings, but my parents' marriage had become so fragile that I didn't dare to leave George on his own for a summer. Plus, I didn't want to lose my valuable job at the Continental. Having become aware of my efficiency, the management had begun, more and more frequently, to allow me to wait on table. This meant tips, in addition to salary.

I would go directly from school to the hotel. Tablecloths would need to be laid, and place settings arranged. The kitchen was a beehive of activity. The staff would have to be fed before the dining room opened, usually supping on osso bucco or pasta of some kind. "Mange, mange, Bastontino!" the chef would sing. At the end of the evening, when the last of the paying customers had left and the tables had been cleared, I would sit in the hotel kitchen and do my homework (as much of it as I could bear to do). Then, I would head for home, and turn in to get some sleep, in preparation for the next day's activities.

In the autumn of that year, after I had turned sixteen, my father apparently felt that I was now old enough to look after myself. So he announced to me (and incidentally to his wife) that he had secured a job where he "could make some real money." This job would require his moving far away to the island of Adak, in the Aleutians. He would be leaving (for how long he had no idea) in just over a week, and would be working as a civilian employee of the army. The announcement arrived like a bombshell. Marian sobbed; George stormed.

I, on the other hand, took the news with equanimity, and quietly began preparing to become the man of the house. I would save my mother. I rose each morning, showered, applied Brilliantine to my hair and combed it, every strand in place. I wore a tie and jacket to school. I called my mother from the payphone in the hallway off the Continental's basement each evening, to assure her that I would be home. I asked whether she would like me to bring something for her to eat, from the kitchen. I wrote the number of the payphone down on a slip of paper and gave it to her.

"Call me when you need anything," I told her. "They'll get me a message." I believed with all my heart, that if I were allowed to captain the ship, it would not sink. I felt reborn. I had boundless energy. Despite my long days of school and work, I completed my homework assignments. My positive attitude showed at Cambridge Latin, and I was elected president of my home room.

On the morning of the day George departed, I said goodbye to my father, and left for school. I phoned my mother that evening from work, but the call was not answered. I arrived home after work, carrying a paper bag with a croissant in it for her breakfast. She was not there to receive it. I went to sleep in my inside room, the weather having turned chilly. At midnight I was awakened by the sound of a slamming door and raucous laughter. I opened my own door a crack, and saw my mother teetering up the stairs on the arm of a man she had clearly picked up at the Elite. I went back to bed and pulled a pillow over my head, hoping to shut out the sounds from my parents' bedroom.

For the next five nights, the scene was repeated with different players. I was devastated. On the sixth night, I returned from work, and found my mother in the kitchen, dressed in her nightgown, sitting at the oil-cloth covered table.

"Couldn't find anybody?" I asked with a sneer. She burst into tears and ran into her bedroom. I felt only coldness in my heart, which I hated, but could do nothing to relieve. I sat down at the table. In a little while, my mother came back and stood in the doorway. I looked at her. In spite of everything, she still seemed to me the most beautiful woman in the world.

"Dallas," she whispered. "Won't you come to bed with me?" What she said hit me like a thunderbolt. I was dumbstruck, could think of no answer to give.

"Please," she said. "I'm so lonely. I can't stand to be alone... please, Dallas." The shape of her body showed through the nightgown. I felt a stirring in my sixteen year old loins. A voice inside me screamed YES. Then I thought of Circe from The Odyssey, and another silent voice whispered: "If you do this, you'll never escape; you'll be trapped forever." A cold self-protective rage took me over.

"No," I said and, getting up from the table, I walked to my room and locked the door. Through the night, I heard the muffled sound of my mother's sobs.

———

The next day was Saturday. I rose early and packed my belongings in a canvas bag. I had noticed a sign on a house not far away, which advertised a furnished room for rent. I walked to the house, carrying my bag, and spoke to the lady who answered the door. Seeing my age, she looked at me dubiously.

"It's alright," I told her confidently. "I've got a good job and plenty of money." I flashed my wad. The landlady took me up two flights and showed me the room. It was sunny and clean, with white walls, a white bedspread on the bed, a chest of drawers and a bed table with a reading lamp on it. A bathroom was just down the hall. The rent was six dollars a week. I handed her the money and moved in.

"It's clean," I told myself, pleased with the room. "It's white and clean." I felt a great relief. I walked up Mass Ave to Sears Roebuck, and bought myself an alarm clock and a small radio. When I got back, I put the radio on the bedside table next to the lamp, plugged it into the wall socket, and turned it on. It was a Philco; I was in the chips. I lay on the bed for the rest of the day listening to war news. That night, I went to work at the Continental. Business was good; the dining room was full. I gave extra good service and got generous tips. The next day, once again I listened to the radio. Fred Allen and Jack Benny were on that night, and I was glad I didn't have to work on Sundays. On Monday I went to school. Nobody knew about my new living arrangements.

They didn't know at work either. On Thursday of that week, it was my mother's forty fifth birthday. I thought about calling her but decided against it. I had made a clean break, and better to leave it that way. She was probably with one of her bums from the bar anyway. Business was light at the hotel, and I finished work early. I moved into the kitchen, sat down at a table and took out my school books. One of the assistant cooks appeared at the far end of the room.

"Hey kid," he yelled. "There's a call for you on the pay phone on the stairs." I knew who it was; no-one else had the number. I stood up from the table and walked passed the chef, who was in the process of shutting down the fire and scraping the grill. I entered the stairwell and picked up the receiver, which had been left dangling on its cord.

"Yeah?"

"It'sh your mother, Dallas." She slurred her words.

"Yeah, I know. What do you want?"

"Won't you please come over, Dallas. It's my birthday."

"No," I said. "You're drunk."

"I know but please. I'm so very..." I hung up the phone. I felt nothing but icy cold. It had been too many years. I picked up my books, thinking to hell with the homework, left the hotel and walked back to my clean white room.

In the morning, my alarm clock woke me and I got up, went down the hall to the bathroom, and brushed my teeth. I took a shower, toweled off and got dressed. If I had asked myself what I felt, which I did not, the answer would no doubt have been *nothing*. I picked up my school books, left the room, went down the stairway and walked out of the house. I stopped at the Economy Cafeteria and ate a half a grapefruit and a toasted English muffin with margarine and grape jelly. Mr. Economy, the owner, was a Greek who had shortened his name from Economakis, hoping it would make him sound more American. He smiled at me and wished me a pleasant day. I strode through Harvard yard as I did every morning, passing the statue of the founder of the college. I climbed the steps of Cambridge Latin, and entered the main hallway, along with other kids, walking on the dark polished wood floor past the statue of Diana.

Entering my classroom, I sat down at my desk and shoved the books I'd brought with me into the space under the writing surface. A few minutes went by. The door opened, and a young woman walked in. I recognized her as a secretary who worked in the principal's office. She approached the teacher, Miss Baldwin, and whispered in her ear. Miss Baldwin looked at me.

"Dallas," she said. "Mr. Downey would like to see you." I stood up and walked through the classroom door. I passed the statue of Diana for the second time that morning. I arrived at the principal's office. The young woman who had delivered the message to Miss Baldwin, asked me to take a seat; she said that Mr. Downey would see me in a moment. As she delivered this message, I noticed that she avoided my eyes. I moved to the bench by the side wall and glanced out the window in time to see a police car moving away from the front of the school.

Mr. Downey opened the inner door of his office and spoke. "Come in, please, Dallas." I rose from the bench and entered the inner sanctum. I'd been there before, usually because of complaints from teachers. Mr. Downey asked me to take a chair. Then he sat down behind his desk.

"Well Dallas, I don't know how else to say this. Your mother is dead." I could hear the old Seth Thomas clock ticking on the principal's wall. Time seemed to slow down. I felt it was incumbent upon me to say something, that it was my turn to move the conversation forward.

"How did she...how did it happen?"

"The police told me that she apparently..." Mr. Downey paused for a moment. I felt sorry for him, wished I could say something to relieve the tension. "Apparently she turned on the gas and put her head in the oven. The neighbors smelled it and called the police. It was just a matter of luck that the place didn't blow up."

"Sorry," I said. The irrelevance of the remark seemed to hang there in the air, and more or less provided a conclusion to the conversation.

Orson Bean

"If you'd like, you're more than welcome to take the rest of the day off." I thanked him. We shook hands and I left the inner office. As I passed the young woman who had delivered the news to my teacher, she didn't look up from the paper she was working on.

I took my time walking home that morning... home to 12 Wright Street. I used my key to enter the front door, climbed the stairs and walked into the kitchen. The police had taken my mother's body away, and there was a printed form sitting on the table saying that it could be found at the Delaney Funeral Home. It gave the address. I looked around the room. The oven door was still open and in front of it, on the floor, were an old army blanket, which I had sometimes used on the back porch, and a pillow. I guessed that she had wanted to be comfortable when she lay down in front of the oven. I wondered if the pillow had lain on top of the open oven door, and had fallen off when the cops had moved her body. I folded the army blanket, and put it on the chair to the left of the catch-all. I lay the pillow on top of it.

The place wasn't too much of a mess. Not knowing what else to do, I left the house and went to the First National. There were empty cardboard boxes stacked out back, and I collected some of those and took them home with me. I went down to the cellar and brought up some old newspapers. Then I began packing stuff for storage. The cops had notified my aunt, and she had called my grandparents.

Marian had written a suicide note saying that her husband had left, her son would not come to see her on her birthday, and that it was too hard to go on. The note somehow made it onto the pages of the Daily Record, a local tabloid.

66

In a few days, there was a small service at Delaney's. Marian looked beautiful, laid out in her coffin. The mortician had done a good job. A friend of hers named Agnes O'Brien came. My grandfather traveled down to say goodbye to his beloved daughter. He didn't say anything to me. My aunt smiled at me, and told me I looked nice in my tie and jacket. Her husband was still tending to wounded soldiers and sailors in the south Pacific. She offered to let me come and live with her, which I did, becoming a baby sitter for her two young children, Phillip and Joyce.

VIII

Nine months later, George returned. He said they'd screwed him over; he had expected to make some real money. When Marian died, I had written to him. I got no answer for weeks. Mail service to and from the Aleutian Islands, with a war going on, was operating at a snail's pace. A response finally came. "My poor boy," the letter began. He never explained what work he was doing for the government, but hinted that good fortune lay in store for him. But months later, in the final note I received, George said that he'd had the bad luck to fall into the hands of a pair of con artists who had convinced him to hand over the money he'd saved, promising to double, maybe triple it. He had done so, and the swindlers and the savings had disappeared. George became disgusted with the people he was working with, quit his job, and ultimately showed up back in Cambridge.

With war still raging in the Pacific, plenty of work was available to men not serving at the front. George applied for, and was given a job working for Harvard College. The campus was so huge and sprawling, that the university maintained its own police force. George became a uniformed yard cop. He was able to rent a small apartment in Harvard Square. It was upstairs over a Hayes-Bickford cafeteria, and had formerly served as student housing. When he'd been back a week and gotten settled, he phoned me at the hotel, and suggested that I move in with him. I knew that Hayes Bickford. It was on Mass Ave not far from The Harvard Coop where, years before, I had purchased my Latin-English dictionary.

I made a date to see my father, and walked to the square. I turned the corner at Holyoke Street, found the entrance to the apartments above the restaurant, and opened the door. There was a small vestibule with a list of tenants on the wall, and a doorbell next to each name. I pushed the buzzer beside my father's name, to let him know I was on the way up. As I climbed the stairs, I noticed something strange. The walls looked red. So did the stairs and windows. Everything had a red tinge to it. Years later, I lay on a psychiatrist's couch, and the doctor pointed out the obvious. "You were furious at him," he said. "Where do you think expression 'seeing red' comes from?"

The apartment was on the fourth floor. George was standing at the open door. He let me in. We did not shake hands. The flat was tiny. There was a twin bed against one wall of the main room, and a couch against another. A table and two wooden chairs stood between a pair of smallish windows, which looked out on Mass Ave, and the college campus beyond. The sound of passing street cars drifted up from the avenue below. A miniscule anteroom stood between the main room and an even smaller bathroom. The anteroom contained a tiny fridge with a hot plate on top of it.

A four foot long tub practically filled the bathroom. A rubber hose with a shower nozzle at the end of it ran from the tub's faucet to a metal fixture which held it overhead. There was a sink with a narrow glass shelf over it, and a medicine cabinet above that. A drinking glass with several used double-edged Gillette razor blades stood on the shelf. George believed that he could sharpen the blades by rubbing them back and forth on the inside of the tumbler. This way, he convinced himself, he would never have to buy new ones. He wore tiny pieces of toilet paper on his face, where he had cut himself shaving.

George offered me one of the wooden chairs and sat in the other one. He asked me how I was doing. I said that I was doing fine. We sat at the table and made small talk. As we did so, I looked at my father, and wondered what on earth he could have been thinking, nine months earlier, to have left a sixteen year old boy in charge of a suicidal, alcoholic woman. When there came a lull in the conversation, George repeated the invitation he had made on the phone, that I should move in with him. Perhaps hoping to hold on to what family I had, I agreed to do so.

I said goodbye to my aunt, thanked her and moved in with my father. The atmosphere in the shared flat on Mass Ave and Holyoke Street was tense, but manageable. I slept on the couch.

⸺•⸺

Through a professor he met at the college, George made arrangements to take a test. It was one which the department of psychology routinely gave to its students. Subsequently, he received the following letter in the mail. Proud of it, he folded it up and carried in his wallet for the rest of his life.

HARVARD UNIVERSITY
Department of Psychology

To Whom It May Concern:

This is to certify that Mr. George F. Burrows scored in the 99.6th percentile on the Guilford-Zimmerman Verbal Comprehension Test. In order to achieve a score in this percentile, Mr. Burrows correctly answered 74 of the 75 items on this test. The time limit on this test is normally 25 minutes. Mr. Burrows achieved his score during a period of ten minutes.

A score in this percentile indicates that Mr. Burrows is superior in verbal comprehension to 99.6% of the college students in the standardization group (a representative sample of the college population).

Robert L. Munroe, Examiner

Based on the results of the test, George was able to join the organization known as MENSA. He began attending the meetings of the local chapter and befriended uber-intellectuals like Norbert Weiner, the great mathematician from M.I.T. With his cop's uniform, he became a sort of mascot at the meetings, an interesting oddity among the elite intelligentsia who made up the group.

In August of '45, the Americans dropped A bombs on Hiroshima and Nagasaki, and the war in the Pacific came to an end. I was selling newspapers at the subway kiosk in Harvard Square. The headlines in the Globe were huge. People had tears in their eyes. I met up with Parker that night in Boston, and we roamed the city as part of the celebratory crowd. Both of us had another year to go in high school.

Despite my indifference to the educational process, I managed to get through my senior year. On Talent Night at Cambridge Latin, I performed an illusion which I had procured at Holden's: the Floating Light Bulb. Carrying a table lamp onto the darkened stage, I unscrewed the bulb, which remained lit. The bulb then flew around the stage, passing through a hoop I held. It got a big hand from the students. At a Celebration of Literature event, I recited a poem which I had committed to memory: Pigs Is Pigs by Ellis Parker Butler. It was a comic piece about the rabbit-like tendency of guinea pigs to multiply (titters from the kids). Written (and performed) in a cheap vaudeville Irish dialect, the narration referred to guinea pigs as dago pigs. I was reprimanded but not expelled.

I met a girl named Ruthie, who was in my class, and she became my first love. She was pretty and vivacious, and I was nuts about her.

Ruthie lived alone with her father in the Fresh Pond neighborhood where I had spent a portion of my youth. George acquired a girlfriend too. Her name was Isabel Hickey and she was president of the New England Astrological Association. George took up with her after becoming interested in that arcane pseudo-science. He had attended a meeting at which she was the main speaker, and introduced himself.

Isobel was the antithesis of Marian. A plain looking woman of George's age, she had a genuine sweetness to her. When I met her, I liked her at once. Isabel was a psychic. She invited Ruthie and me to her house for a séance. Sitting around a card table, the three of us placed our hands on top of it. Isabel went into some kind of a trance, and asked if there was "anyone there." There was. The spirit who came through was that of an eighteen year old sailor who had died under terrifying conditions on the Squalus, a U.S. Navy submarine, which had sunk off Portsmouth, N.H. in 1939. The young man spoke through Isabel Hickey's voice, and Ruthie was quite moved. Then the card table began shaking, and finally hopped violently around the room, followed by the three of us. We had to move quite swiftly to keep up with it. With my then substantial knowledge of how things were faked, I could see no trickery involved.

Isabel predicted that if I did not buckle down and do my homework, I would not graduate in the spring of '46. I did not see how it took a psychic to foretell that. My plan was to do the bare minimum of work needed to get my diploma. I felt that the school and its teachers had nothing worthwhile left to impart to me. I knew how to read and write, and the rest of it I would handle myself as the need arose. When graduation time arrived, the students at Cambridge High and Latin were told they would be allowed only two pairs of guest tickets each, because the auditorium was quite small. One pair of seats would be downstairs, the other pair up in the balcony. To show his displeasure with my apparent lack of ambition, George told me that he would use the upstairs pair, and that I could do what I wanted with the better tickets.

———•———

There was a teacher named Miss Hartigan, a splendid old bird who taught what was called Forensics. (public speaking, debating, etc.) She took a shine to me; I was managing to sublimate my class-clown tendencies into somewhat more useful exercises. She directed me in poetry readings and dramatic dissertations. When I graduated (by the skin of my teeth), I sat on the stage of the high school auditorium in the front row with the honors winners, because Miss Hartigan had seen to it that I was given the Forensic Award. As prize recipients came forward to accept their trophies, I was among them. After the ceremony, George was furious.

"If I'd known you were getting some kind of award, I'd have sat downstairs," he complained. I had the grace not to smirk.

That night, to celebrate, I hooked up with my friend Parker and we took the subway to Revere Beach, the Coney Island of Boston. In addition to the usual thrill rides, there was a splendid freak show there. I enjoyed this offering and remembered fondly, for the rest of my life, Albert-Alberta, the half man-half woman, and Schlitzie the "pin head" girl who had starred with the Hilton Sisters (the famous Siamese twins) in Todd Browning's production of the movie Freaks.

IX

Parker and I decided that we would join the army together. We both turned eighteen the summer after graduation (1946), and it was possible to get one's service obligations out of the way in those days, with a minimal enlistment of eighteen months. Both of us, it seemed, were happy enough to get away from home. Friends derided our decision, saying that the war was over and that there was never going to be another draft. A lot of them, not too far down the road, were sent to Korea for long, miserable years.

Parker and I met up at a recruiting center in Kenmore Square in Boston. The sergeant in charge greeted us with a broad smile, telling us how patriotic we were for enlisting. Later, it would occur to me that that would be the last time a non-commissioned officer would smile at me for many months. We had three days before we were to meet at a bus depot for transport to our induction center at Fort Dix, N.J. I shook my father's hand and received a nice hug from Isobel Hickey. I spent a tearful and loving evening with Ruthie, and then Parker and I reconnoitered at the bus station.

When we disembarked at Fort Dix, it was all business. We stripped down and were given a physical, turning our heads to cough. We were issued fatigues and boots, which we donned, and basic equipment, like a canteen and mess kit. Everything was jammed into duffel bags, and we were shown to a barracks, where we would spend the night, before finding out the destination to which we'd be shipped in the morning, for basic training. We selected bunks in the barracks, and stowed our duffel bags at the foot of the bunk. Then a sergeant ordered us to "fall out" in front of the barracks. We did so, and the sergeant proceeded to castigate us as a sorry looking bunch of misfits. I smirked and turned to whisper something to Parker. The sergeant caught me.

"You," he cried. "Take one step forward and let us know what's so damn funny!" I moved forward.

"Well, Sarge..." I smiled.

"Shut your mouth," cried the sergeant. "Now look at me. Do you see this finger where it's pointing?" I said that I did.

"My finger is pointing at the mess hall over yonder. Now walk on over there and introduce yourself. Tell them that you're the loser that sergeant sent over to clean the grease traps. Do you get me?" I said that I did.

"On the double, then." I hustled to the mess hall. I found the non-com in charge, and introduced myself as instructed. Eight hours went by. I had cleaned the grease traps, and then re-cleaned them, upon being informed that I had done as piss-poor a job as any recruit the non-com had ever seen. I was finally released and told to return to my barracks and not show my miserable face in those parts again.

Exhausted, my newly issued fatigues covered with grease, I stumbled out of the mess hall and headed in the direction of the barracks in which I had stowed my gear. When I entered the hall, I was sure I had made a mistake. I walked out again and looked around. No other barracks was nearby. I walked back in. The barracks was empty. No one and nothing were there. My duffel bag, which had contained everything I owned in the world, was gone. The mattresses on the rows of cots had been folded back on themselves, so that springs were showing on the bottom half of each one. I went outside again. It was dark. I had left my wrist watch in the duffel bag along with my wallet and the paperwork the army had issued me, so I had no idea what time it was. I walked back over to the mess hall, where I'd spent hours working. It was closed up by then and no one was there.

Not knowing what else to do, I returned to the empty barracks. I unfolded one of the mattresses, and positioned the one from the next cot on top of it. Crawling between the two mattresses I attempted to keep warm. At the age of eighteen, I was too old to cry, but couldn't keep a few tears from rolling down my cheeks. I wondered what had happened to Parker. I had never felt so lonely in my life. Finally I managed to drift off to sleep. I was awakened in the middle of the night by a terrible dream. My mother's hand reached out to me from the soft earth of a freshly dug grave. I was terrified. I shivered under my mattress, both from the cold and the dream. Finally, I was able to get back to sleep.

At the crack of dawn, a sergeant poked his head in the door of the supposedly empty barracks. He spotted me under my mattress.

"Who the hell are you?" he cried. "Who in the name of holy, sweet Jesus Christ, our beloved Lord and Savior, are you? And why are you here be-spoiling the army's good clean mattresses with that greasy set of fatigues?" I hopped out of bed and stood at what I believed to be attention.

"Sir," I began.

"Shut up," cried the sergeant. "Shut your pie hole. You do not call me sir. I am a non–commissioned officer, not an officer, and you do not address a non-commissioned officer with the title sir. Do you understand me?"

"Yes, sir,"

"WHAT?!"

"Sorry sergeant"

"Now. Please enlighten me as to what in the name of all that's holy you are doing here, looking as though you'd just spent eight hours cleaning grease traps?" I explained to the sergeant that I had been told to put all my possessions into a duffel bag, and then ordered to muster out in front of the barracks. And that was the last I had seen of the duffel bag, and all that was in it.

"So, you fourteen-karat gold brick, the truth is you don't know who you are."

"No, sergeant. I do know who..."

"But you have no papers that show who you are. So as far as the army is concerned, you don't know who you are." The sergeant took me to an administrative office. Each new member of the armed forces whom I met was equally disgusted at the condition and situation in which I found myself. There were no computers in those days, so it took hours and many phone calls to figure out just who the poor lost recruit was, and how to deal with me. Finally, new documents and equipment were issued, I was hooked up with a group of enlistees who had arrived from Philadelphia and, a day later, I was sent by train to Fort Knox, Kentucky. It took me a month to find out what had happened to Parker, who had been shipped to a camp in Texas, and spent the eighteen months of his enlistment learning how to be a cook.

Fort Knox, where the gold is, was where I was to spend my next two months in basic training. On the day I arrived, I was shown to a barracks, which would be my home for the period. Then, as in Fort Dix, my fellow recruits and I were told to line up outside for further instructions. It apparently being my karma to do so, I made a wise crack to the kid next to him. The sharp-eyed sergeant caught me.

"You, what's your name?" I told him my name.

"Well, *Dallas*, whatever the hell kind of name that is, let's see you give us twenty five pushups." After eighteen, my arms began to quiver.

"Alright, pansy boy. Fall in and we'll try you again tomorrow."

I would later describe my basic training as "a living heck." Not so terrible really, but bad enough to complain about. I was taught to make my bed "so tight that a quarter will bounce on it." I was issued a carbine, taught how to shoot it and, upon finishing my basic training, given a marksman medal to pin on my military blouse. I was taught to load big shells into howitzers. My barracks group "screwed up" in some manner, and we were all awaked at two A.M. and told to G.I. the floor (scrub it) with toothbrushes. After a month, I received a weekend pass, and took a bus into Louisville, where I wandered the street forlornly, fantasizing that in my uniform I would attract the eye of a beautiful young woman. Donna Reed was the one I had in mind. I attracted no-one and returned to the base early.

When basic training was over, I was given ten day's leave and told that at the end of it I was to report to a base in San Francisco. I took a train to Boston and moved back in with George. Isobel Hickey marveled over how I looked in my uniform. I had lost eight pounds and was fit and trim. Ruthie cried and hugged me. I took her out for a Coke, glancing around to see if people were noticing me in my khakis. When I had three days left to my leave, I enquired at Boston army headquarters as to how I was supposed to get to San Francisco. I was told that I could get there any way I wanted, but that a "troop train" left every night from South Station, and that that would be free.

The troop train was from hell. I slept sitting up on a hard banquette. There was no food available. The train would stop at a town for twenty minutes, and soldiers would dash out and try to find potato chips or the makings of a sandwich, and then re-board the train. Occasionally, a G.I. would miss the departure and have to wait twenty four hours for the next troop train. I arrived in San Francisco and hailed a cab, asking the driver to take me to the departure center on the bay, from which I would catch a ship to somewhere in the Pacific. The cab driver handed me a business card. It read "McGee's Hotel: Where you can always get in." The driver winked at me.

Arriving at the departure center, I was shown my bunk, and told that I had another free night if I wanted it, and could go into San Francisco. I hailed another cab and asked to be taken to the address on the business card. A sweet Black hooker took me to her room. I lay with her, thought of Ruthie, and was introduced to the mysteries of carnal knowledge. Afterwards, I celebrated with a beer at the White Rose Bar, and then took another cab back to the base. In the morning, I joined a huge throng of soldiers on a wharf. Several hundred men in front of me were sent to Korea. The ship bound for Seoul filled up, and I waited while it sailed and another one docked. This ship, I was told, would head for Yokohama. It was late December, a few days before Christmas.

The ship was a converted cargo vessel. The compartment in which I found myself billeted, was next to the mess. I was assigned the bottom hammock of four, so there were three G.I.s stacked above me. The ship headed north, preparing to sail along the Aleutian Islands. I wondered if I would be able to spot Adak. When the ship left the harbor, the seas became choppy. Then, they became rough. My face turned green. Soldiers all around me were seasick. The smell of food being cooked next door was unendurable. I stumbled out of my hammock, and made it up to the deck. G.I.s were throwing up into the ocean. I joined them. It was freezing cold. I made it back down to my hammock.

The trip to Japan, I was told, would take five days. The ship rose up on the crests of waves, then slammed down, then rose up again and slammed down. The first three days, I was afraid I was going to die; the last two days, I was afraid I wasn't going to die. At meal times, the sailors who ran the ship, their sea legs intact, and the few soldiers who had the good fortune not to be seasick, lined up in front of my hammock, waiting to get into the mess, to eat my food as well as theirs. Mealtime after mealtime this happened, and I began to hate them for the unforgivable crime of not being sick. How I despised them, as they whistled cheerfully past my hammock. Decades later, I recognized that look of hatred on people's faces, when I was feeling happy, and the people glaring at me were not.

There was a stack of oranges just inside the mess hall. I smelled these oranges night and day until, like Pavlov's dog, the smell of oranges began to nauseate me. At night, they showed a movie on deck, the sixteen millimeter film projected onto a sail secured between two masts. The movie was Kiss of Death starring Richard Widmark. Somebody had screwed up and stowed just one flick on board for the entire trip. On each of the five nights of the trip, I hobbled up, lay down on the hard deck, froze, and watched the picture. I came to know Widmark's performance by heart. Brian Donleavey was my favorite of the supporting players. On Christmas Eve, December 24th, the crew passed out little gifts to each G.I., courtesy of the Red Cross. Each small cardboard box contained a cookie, a tube of toothpaste and a toothbrush. I ate the cookie. Sometime during the night, the ship crossed the International Date Line, and in the morning, when everybody woke up, it was December 26th.

We arrived in Yokohama. A tent city had been set up. I was shown a bunk and told to go and eat lunch in the mess tent. There was pile of oranges just inside the entrance. I smelled them, stepped out side the tent and upchucked. After two days in Yokohama, the group I was assigned to, took a train and traveled to a town called Koi Zumi, fifty miles north of Tokyo. As we passed through the outskirts of the capitol, I looked out the train window and saw that for miles around Tokyo, nothing was left standing but smokestacks. There was not a building in sight. Tokyo had been firebombed, around the clock, twenty four hours a day, in an attempt to break the Japanese people's spirit. At the base of each chimney, a little hut had been built of scrap metal or bits of wood. A surviving family would be living in each of these, and as they cooked their dinner, a tiny wisp of smoke would come out the top of the smoke stack far above.

At Koi Zumi, the troops were billeted in what had been an aircraft factory. I slept in one of twenty bunks in the factory's office. As an occupying soldier, I practiced loading the big howitzers, as I had learned to do in basic training. I drew guard duty every few weeks. Guard duty lasted twenty four hours: four hours marching around the base carrying a carbine, and two hours off, in a bunk... not enough time to get any sleep. A G.I. from New York, named Cuccarella, had pulled a nice gig, running the base movie theater. I hooked up with him, and got to put on some talent shows. These were really just an excuse to perform my magic act, which I did as often as possible for the troops. (I had contrived to carry my apparatus, the change bag and a new illusion, the Zombie ball, along with me on the trip to Japan.) The act was coming along nicely. I wrote letters to Parker every week, back in Texas, and learned that he was keeping up with his magic too. I drew K.P. periodically, mostly peeling potatoes and scrubbing pots.

Japanese currency was worthless. American cigarettes became the medium of exchange, at least in the part of Japan I was visiting. Each U.S. soldier was allowed to purchase a carton a week of Camels or Luckies. These could be traded with the locals, who then traded them with one another.

Stars and Stripes, the daily newspaper of the military, told of unreconstructed Nazi sharp shooters in Germany, who still hid on rooftops and picked off occupying American soldiers, long after Germany had surrendered. Life was very different in Japan. When the Emperor had instructed the Japanese people to surrender to General MacArthur, they had obeyed him implicitly. On the couple of times that I was able to get into Tokyo (I had befriended a lieutenant, who took me along in his Jeep when he had leave), I found that I could walk down the darkest of streets late at night with no fear.

———·•·———

Japan was devastated. In the final days of the war, the fascist government, unable to import oil, had used firewood to run their equipment. In a desperate attempt to keep from surrendering (even though they surely knew the war was lost) they had cut down all the trees in the mountains around Koi Zumi. When the annual spring rains came, there were no roots to keep the land on the mountains from sliding. Local villages were inundated with mud. I saw bodies floating past the base.

On the day that I enlisted, I automatically became a Buck Private. When a Buck Private completes his basic training, he is promoted, pro forma, to the rank of Private First Class. In the army, if a Private First Class does anything whatsoever of value, he is promoted to the rank of Corporal or T5. Conversely, if he screws up, he is demoted back to Buck Private. For a soldier to complete his term of enlistment as a Private First Class means that he has not been noticed. That had been my goal, and I achieved it.

X

Back home, as an honorably discharged veteran, I became a member of the 52/20 club. This meant that every week for a year the government sent me a check for twenty bucks. That wasn't bad in 1948. A burger at the White Tower was a nickel. A grilled cheese and a Pepsi at the lunch counter in the drug store cost fifteen cents. I did not want to live with George again. Instead, I checked into a theatrical rooming house in Boston. It was called The Warrenton, and was near the dog pound where I had found Homer. The rent was $9 a week.

The place was pretty seedy. An old lady with one leg sat at a front desk in the rundown lobby. Down-at-the-heel performers stayed there while working local clubs. My room was on the second floor. The bed was lumpy. Paint peeled off the walls. The light bulbs were 40 watt. The room next to mine was occupied by a dog act. The dogs got home from their job at one in the morning and yapped until their master fed them. But at least I had privacy. I had begun seeing Ruthie again.

There was a somewhat classier theatrical boarding place a few blocks away. It was called the Carleton House and cost

$11 a week. I was determined that as soon as I could afford it I would move there.

By the time I returned from Japan, I had developed a fairly professional magic act. I opened by making a rubber canary in a collapsible cage disappear up my sleeve (it looked better than it sounds) and concluded the act by rolling up sheets of newspaper, tearing them and fashioning a six foot tall "paper Eucalyptus tree." (Years later, I performed this trick on Broadway in a musical review called John Murray Anderson's Almanac.)

I began making the rounds of local theatrical booking agents trying to get work in nightclubs. At that time, before people owned TV sets, they still went out in the evening. There was a full year's work to be had in working class clubs throughout New England, some full weeks, mostly weekends. The weekend gigs would pay $15 a night. There were several agencies that provided acts for local night clubs. The largest of these was the Ford Agency. It booked shows into a few spots in the city (the top notch clubs, those which featured names like Milton Berle and Desi Arnaz, got their talent from New York). It also booked shows in a great many surrounding towns, some as far away as Maine and New Hampshire. I was not yet known enough in the business for the Ford Agency to pay attention to me. But through some of the lesser agencies, I was able to get weekend gigs in places like the Kiwanis Club in Marlboro, and the Veterans of Foreign Wars Hall in Saugus ("Fri. Sat. Sun. Three Big Acts Three. Direct From Boston").

I lucked into a full week job at a joint in Boston. It was called Hurley's Log Cabin, and it was there that I underwent a change of name. I knew that if I were to have any future in the business, I would eventually have to drop the hocus pocus and switch to stand-up. I was already interspersing comedy with the tricks, but my humor was not suitable for the clubs I was working in. I had devised a mock historical spiel, which I delivered while rolling up the sheets of newspaper to build my tree. It was inspired by the lectures George had given on our meanders. "In ancient Rome, the more sophisticated citizens would not patronize the Coliseum, where they threw people to the lions. Those of 'the narrow lapel toga' would go to the fashionable east side of Rome, to smaller, more intimate coliseums, where they threw midgets to chickens. It was a terrible way to go: pecked to death."

I had a crew cut and wore a three button, grey flannel suit. My opening line at Hurley's was, "My name is Dallas Burrows. Harvard '48 (pause) Yale nothing." The response was nil. A deathly stillness would be broken by cries of, "Bring out the stripper!" Only the musicians in the band laughed. The piano player, whose name was Val duVal, suggested that the reason the act was getting no laughs was not just because I was "too hip for the room," the general conclusion of musicians wherever I worked. It was also, he said, because the act didn't start off right; the opening joke didn't work.

"And that," he concluded, "is because you don't have a funny name." He told me to try the name of Roger Duck.

The next evening, I walked out onto the stage at Hurley's and said, "Good evening. My name is Roger Duck. Harvard '48... Yale nothing." The silence was profound. The piano player did not give up. The following night his suggestion was Orson Bean (pretentious first name, silly second name. Funny, he reasoned). I was game. I introduced myself, for the first time, as Orson Bean. The Harvard-Yale joke got a laugh, and to my surprise and delight, so did the rest of my jokes. Val du Val had been right. As luck would have it, a local booking agent, a fat guy named Bozo Zimbel, was in the audience that night. Bozo was a minor agent with the Ford group. After the show, he came backstage to my dressing room (a nail).

"You're alright, kid," he said. "I got a full week's work for you in Montreal." I was excited.

"What's the money?"

"Eighty five dollars less ten percent. And you gotta pay your own traveling and living expenses."

My jaw dropped. "It will cost me more than that to *do* it."

"Well, you gotta save up for these gigs!"

I accepted the job, and kept the name of Orson Bean. The club in Montreal turned out to be French speaking. The audience didn't understand the jokes, but the magic did okay. I stayed in a small hotel near the club. It was mid-winter and Montreal was thrillingly beautiful. A whole section of the city was not plowed out for the season and was accessible only by horse drawn sleigh. I did the best I could for the week's engagement, translating my jokes into the French I had learned as a kid. They were too hip pour la chambre. At least, that's what I told myself. When the gig was over I took the train back to Boston, passing the city of my birth on the way.

Some of the jobs I got were grim. At a club in Medford, I found myself on the bill with an act called Hermione's Midgets. Hermione was an English drunk, unshaven and overweight. He wore a threadbare tuxedo which had fit him once but was now too tight. He sported white socks inside his black, patent leather shoes (to accommodate his bad feet). The Midgets were four foul-tempered and aromatic dwarves. The act, which opened the show, consisted of twenty minutes of knock-about, so-called comedy which involved the little men insulting Hermione, and Hermione taking mock umbrage. The act may have worked in a Variety Hall in Leeds, but in the closer confines of a nightclub in Massachusetts, it got few laughs and rarely received more than a smattering of applause.

But the worst of it came when their performance was over. The dwarves hopped off the dance floor and ran around the club, dunning people to buy miniature bibles for a quarter, rushing from table to table, pulling at their sleeves, insisting that they make a purchase, and reacting nastily to anyone who declined. Watching from the wings, I could see that the audience I was about to inherit was becoming, to put it mildly, unsettled. When the Midgets finally gave up and disappeared through the kitchen door, a voice on the loud-speaker announced, "Now, the magical musings of Orson Bean," and I was on. No laughs.

Another of my rites of passage involved being booked at a state fair in New Hampshire. The performers worked on a grandstand behind a racetrack. The audience sat in automobiles in a parking lot on the far side of the track, where loud speakers had been set up. It was an odd situation. Rather than laughing or clapping to show their appreciation, people honked their horns. My offering was received largely in silence; the paper tree got a few mercy honks.

———•———

One night when I was not working, I went to see a nightclub hypnotist. When the magician, who did not know me, asked for volunteers, I raised my hand. I thought it would be interesting to be hypnotized. I stood on the nightclub floor next to several other audience members. "Your eyes are growing heavy," said the hypnotist. My eyes were not growing heavy, but I didn't want to spoil a fellow performer's act. I feigned "going under." I did what the hypnotist asked. I crowed like a chicken when ordered to do so. The audience laughed and cheered. I was told that when I woke up I would remember nothing that had occurred but would feel calm and refreshed. I pretended to wake up, remember nothing and feel calm and refreshed. The audience gave me a big hand. When I returned to my seat the people at the next table regarded me with wonder. A lady leaned over to speak to me. "What did it feel like?" she asked.

I had a revelation. Perhaps some of the other volunteers were pretending to be hypnotized too. Not going under would make them look like spoilsports and disappoint the crowd. Worse, they would be ignored, as the hypnotist would likely turn to more malleable subjects. Going along with the gag made them celebrities for the night. I decided on a bold course. I needed a new and stronger close to my magic act. I would get volunteers up on stage, see if I could get them to get them to cooperate, and find out what happened.

I was booked into a joint called The Hofbrau in Lowell. With an out-of-town job like this the agent would hire one performer with a car. A typical show in working class clubs like The Hofbrau consisted of a comic, who acted as emcee, a variety act (magician, like me, or ventriloquist or juggler) and a "girl singer". The performers would meet at a pre-arranged location in Boston (usually the corner of Tremont and Boylston) and the owner of the car would collect a dollar fifty from each act "to help with the gas." Actually, it was a nice little windfall for those performers lucky enough to own wheels. The performers would arrive at the club an hour before show time and the singer would pass out her arrangements to the band and have a quick rehearsal on the raised dance floor.

As the customers began to arrive and seat themselves at tables around the stage, I began scouting potential accomplices. I was determined not to ask for volunteers but rather to select people I felt would be failsafe, and I had come up with a method for doing this. The criteria I had decided on for choosing an accomplice was as follows: first rule, men only... never women. When a man falls down, we laugh; when a woman falls down, we rush to help her up. Second rule: average run-of-the-mill looking men only; overly handsome men or overly homely ones tend to be self-conscious about their looks, so are ill-at-ease in the public eye. Third rule: never pick a red-headed guy. They have been made fun of since childhood and are not comfortable with people laughing at them.

It was Friday night of a Fri-Sat-Sun booking. The place filled up pretty well. The emcee opened the show with some standard jokes: "Good evening Ladies and Germs. I'm staying down the block at the Hotel Pocahontas. It's called that because everyone registers under the name of Mr. and Mrs. John Smith. You don't even have to sign the book, they have a rubber stamp. The ceiling in my room is so low the mice are humpbacked. I found a dead cockroach under my bed. I didn't mind that but a hundred of his friends came to the funeral." My heart sank. The comic was getting laughs. That meant the crowd would be unlikely to enjoy my stuff.

The comic introduced the girl singer: "We wanna start off the show with a bang... and here she is!" When the singer was finished, the comic then did his routines, more of the same, and then it was my turn. My humor was greeted with minimal response. As usual the band laughed, for which I was grateful. The audience liked the magic tricks well enough. Then I took a deep breath and announced that I was going to try something the crowd had never seen before: an experiment in psychic thought transmission. I pointed to one of the victims I had pre-selected in my mind before the show.

"You, sir. We have never met, you don't know who I am. Is that correct?" The man acknowledged that this was the case. I looked at the other side of the club and pointed to the second man I had chosen, an average looking sort with a pleasant enough face.

"And you, sir. You don't know me either. Right?" The man concurred. "Would you mind raising your hand so everyone can see who you are?" The pleasant looking man obliged, seemingly happy to have attention called to him. I turned back to my original choice.

"Would you please raise your hand sir." This man complied as well. "Now," I said, "We need a third volunteer. I pointed to a table in the middle of the room. "If you will, sir, raise your hand.

You will act as the battery through which we will transfer a series of thoughts from one side of the room to the other. I could sense that the audience was into this, waiting to see what was about to occur.

"Can you all see my volunteers, folks?" I asked. " Gentlemen, please stand up so everyone can see you. Let's give them a hand, people." The audience obliged. I could see that my selected assistants were enjoying the attention. I had chosen correctly.

"Oh what the hell, let's bring them up on stage," I laughed. "How about it, folks, a big hand for these courageous volunteers." Everyone joined in the laughter, and the three men climbed up onto the dance floor. I announced that instead of thought transference I was going to perform a new type of hypnosis. I asked each volunteer his name and shook his hand. Grasping the elbow of one of the men, I caused his right hand to rise up involuntarily and I shook it again. I did this four or five times more, pretending each time to be surprised. The volunteer began to laugh and the audience laughed along with him. Under cover of the laugh I whispered to my assistant, "It's all a gag. Do what I tell you and we'll have fun."

I gazed into the mans eyes for a moment, then raised his thumb to his nose. The audience laughed. I said into the microphone. "He can't get it off. It's stuck." I turned to the assistant, "Try," I said. "Try with all your might. You cannot remove it." I winked at the man, who, intoxicated by the laughs he was getting, struggled to pull the thumb off his nose. The audience howled. I clapped my hands loudly. "You're free!" I cried, and my assistant pulled his thumb away to loud applause. Turning to the other two accomplices, I told them to shake hands. "You guys should get to know each other," I said. The crowd laughed and I whispered,

"It's all fun. Make like you're stuck." The two men struggled vainly to let go of each other. The audience went nuts. I then told the men to stare straight ahead into the spotlight. I asked the drummer to give me a jungle beat. I raised my hand to wave it in front of the first assistant's face. With my arm as a cover, I whispered, "When I clap my hands, fall down and I'll catch you." Quickly, before the stooge had time to think about it I clapped my hands. The volunteer fell back, I caught him, eased him to the floor and whispered, "You're stuck. You can't get up." The volunteer struggled mightily and couldn't budge from the floor. The audience was going crazy. I repeated the some thing with the two others, then clapped my hands again and said, "You're all free. Stand up!" I asked for a big hand for my assistants, then followed one of them to his table and stuck his hand onto the back of his wife's chair. The audience howled.

"Thanks folks and goodnight." I was off and the cheers were enormous. Back in the dressing room, the MC cornered me.

"Cripes, kid. How did you do that?" he asked.

"It's a little known form of instant hypnosis developed centuries ago by a guy named Mesmer," I answered, reminding myself of Lon Merritt.

Word of my success spread to the Ford Agency, and I began to get booked into a better class of club, for more money. The first thing I did was to move into the Carlton. I said goodbye to the old lady with one leg in the lobby of the Warrenton. She seemed sad to see me go. There was maid service twice a week at the Carlton. And there was a better class of clientele. The extra two bucks rent made a difference.

I decided to avail myself of the services of a personal manager; that was what Fred Mack called himself. His office was on the second floor of a building on Boylston Street, over a Wimpy's Hamburger restaurant. Wimpy's sold a nominally better burger than the White Tower and charged twice as much: a dime. I could afford to patronize Wimpy's now but still preferred, perhaps for old times sake, the five cent burgers at White Tower. Fred Mack had a list of performers who made their headquarters in the Boston area. With the list in front of him he would telephone the Ford Agency and the other smaller outfits, find out which clubs were in need of bookings and suggest his clients. His fee for this was five percent. This was in addition to the ten percent the acts paid to the agency. I decided it was worth fifteen percent of my earnings to avoid having to go from agency to agency and plead for work. I became a client of Fred Mack.

One of the earliest engagements I booked through this new arrangement was a weekend gig in Pawtucket, Rhode Island for $15 a night, a humiliating reversal, but it was all the place would pay and I wanted to keep working. The month was December. The Friday of the job was, as it turned out, Christmas Eve and the Saturday was Christmas. Who would want to go to a cheap nightclub on Christmas Eve, I asked myself? (The question turned out to be prophetic.) The ride belonged to a dance team. Ruthie wanted to be with me on the holiday eve and Fred Mack had enquired of the agency to make sure that the owner of the car would have room for an extra passenger. He had.

I was doing more comedy material now. That was what I wanted to do, and with the insurance of the hypnotism giving me a strong close to the act, I took the opportunity to hone my material, laughs or not. I knew that the band would always support me. So, on this job I was booked as emcee. That meant I had to do "time." The show was supposed to last an hour. The dance team would do two or three spots, adding up to maybe thirteen minutes, the girl singer could be counted on for perhaps twelve and the rest of the hour was up to me.

The little group of players met at Tremont and Boylston at five p.m. and took off for Rhode Island. Ruthie, the girl singer, and I sat in the back of the dance team's sedan and the husband and wife of the dance team sat up front. The traffic was mercifully light and we arrived at the club in plenty of time. We walked in. The boss was a sour looking Portuguese guy. He sat at the end of the bar behind the cash register and, when asked where the dressing rooms were, pointed to a door stage-left of the raised dance floor. It was early and the band had not yet arrived. I told Ruthie she could order a hot turkey sandwich and a Coke. She found a chair at a table in the rear of the room. I sat in the dressing room, trying to figure out how to do enough time to round out the hour. The band arrived and the dance team rehearsed with them. So did the girl singer. I joined Ruthie at her table and held her hand. The show was to begin at nine. As that hour drew near, there was not a single customer in the place. As emcee, I approached the Portuguese guy at the cash register.

"If there's no one here," I asked, "do we still go on?"

"I pay, you make the show," he glared. I went back stage to deliver the news. At nine, the band struck up introductory music and I grabbed the mike and walked to the center of the floor.

"Good evening," I said. "My name is Orson Bean. Harvard '48… Yale nothing." The band did not laugh. I told a few jokes and then brought the dance team out for their first number.

It was a rumba. When they finished, Ruthie applauded from the back of the house. I told a few more jokes, then brought out the singer. She sang five songs and left the stage. Ruthie applauded and the singer came back and did an encore. The dance team came back and performed a fox trot routine. Now it was my turn. I made the canary disappear and my girl friend applauded. The Portuguese guy looked at her and she stopped clapping. I did my comedy bits. The band began to laugh a little. How am I going to do the hypnotism with no one here, I asked myself? How can I do enough time to round out the show?

The front door to the club opened and a man and woman walked in. Who would take his wife to a place like this on Christmas Eve, I wondered? A waitress showed the couple to a table for two by the side wall. I tried to play to them but they didn't look up. It was obvious, even from the stage, that they were having an argument. I went back to playing to the band, trying to get them to laugh. Ruthie tried to help by laughing but every time she did, the Portuguese guy looked at her and she stopped. I approached the portion of my act where I had to find volunteers. The muted sounds of the couple's argument drifted across the dance floor.

The wife from the arguing couple stood up and walked to the bar. I watched her ask the bartender something and saw him point to the entrance to the ladies room. Operating by rote now, I began to talk about mesmerism. I felt like a somnambulist. I turned to the husband, who was the only member of the audience, and asked if we had ever met. He shook his head no. I asked him if he would be good enough to come up onto the stage and participate in an experiment. To my absolute astonishment, he stepped up onto the dance floor and joined me at the microphone. There was now no-one left to play to. I whispered to him that it was all a gag and that he should just go along. The door to the ladies room opened and when the arguing wife returned to her table and saw her husband with his thumb stuck to his nose, she turned her chair around and faced the back of the room.

I finished my act and asked for a big hand for his assistant. There was no one to applaud. I asked for a big hand for the band. I said goodnight, left the stage and went to the dressing room. A moment later, the waitress looked in.

"The boss wants to see you," she said. I walked to the back of the club and approached the owner at the cash register. He looked at me for a minute, then pointed a finger at me and said, "You stink." He handed me two five dollar bills and four ones. "The hot turkey sandwich and the Coke," he explained. "Don't come back tomorrow." The other performers were out of the dressing room by now. Ruthie got up from her table and joined me at the bar. We all got into the car, and drove home to Boston in silence. Ruthie sat close to me. When we arrived at Tremont and Boylston, the husband from the dance team said that he was genuinely sorry to do so, but that he would have to charge an extra dollar fifty for Ruthie's ride. From the fifteen dollars had come three bucks for the gas money and a dollar for the sandwich. There would be a dollar fifty to the agent and seventy five cents to the personal manager. I had been "cancelled" on Christmas Eve and had netted $8.75. I took Ruthie home to Cambridge on the subway, and then rode back to Boston and the Carlton House.

XI

I woke up thinking about my grandfather. I still loved him so much. At the funeral we had not spoken. It was clear that he had, at least in part, blamed me for the death of his daughter. And we'd had no contact since. A little stack of writing paper lay on a table in the Carlton House lobby. I picked up a piece of it, sat down and wrote, "Dear grandmother and grandfather, It's been quite a while since we've seen each other. I'm back from my stint in the army in Japan and would love to come and see you. Please write me at the address on the outside of the envelope and let me know if that would be okay. And send me your phone number, please, as I do not remember it. Dallas." I mailed the letter. A week went by, and I got an answer. "Yes, please come." The phone number was included.

A few days later, I hopped on the bus at the depot in Kenmore Square, not far from the enlistment office where Parker and I had joined the army. I had packed a few clothes and a ham sandwich for the trip. The ride seemed to take forever. I was too nervous to eat the sandwich. I wondered how it would feel to walk up the road to my grandfather's house after all these years. Would the old man be angry when he opened the door to let me in?

The bus pulled into Hartland, made a wide turn around the statue of the Civil War soldier and stopped directly in front of the general store. I grabbed my overnight bag and stepped off. As I did, tears came to my eyes. My grandfather was standing there waiting for me at the bus stop. I looked into his face and saw love and forgiveness. I wanted to throw my arms around him, but it was New England so we shook hands. We walked to the house. It was almost five o'clock, dinner-time in Hartland. And sure enough, when we stepped through the door, my grandmother gave me a hug and then said, "Wash your hands, Dallas. It's time to eat."

We had chicken pie on home-made baking powder biscuits, and, for dessert, blackberry shortcake on home-made baking powder biscuits (the berries from beside the barn). In the few days I stayed I put on a pound and a half. I slept in my old room. Everything about the place moved me almost to tears. I felt as if a huge burden had been lifted from my heart. My grandparents had welcomed me. There was no need to talk about what had happened in the past. Katherine Pollard seemed a bit less reserved than I remembered her as a kid. And my grandfather was his old ebullient self.

I wandered through the house. The warm and inviting middle room had always been my favorite. Oil paintings of "the ancestors" adorned the walls. These, I had learned as a boy, were painted in the previous century by itinerant artists in exchange for a few nights' room and board from whoever had owned the place at the time. I remembered summer Sunday afternoons in that room, when friends of the Pollards would come to call. They would sit with a pitcher of iced tea, grandmother in her rocking chair, grandpa at his desk, the guests on the horse-hair sofa. The clock on the wall would tick and every so often somebody would say something.

"Ever hear from Harriet Miller?"

"No, not for years. Don't know what became of her. (pause) She never married, did she?"

"No. Never married. Had a friend who taught girls' gym at the high school in Windsor. Hmm. Never married. No." Then there might be a lull of five minutes or so while they just sat and enjoyed the stillness and one another's company. When the acquaintances had gone home, grandmother would say to her husband, "Wasn't that a nice visit."

There was a bookcase in the front parlor. I had, as a child, read every volume in it. All the Oz books were there. My favorite had been The Tin Man of Oz. There was a stereoptican viewer and a collection of 3D slides which I knew by heart. My grandmother's old Mah Jong set sat in the bottom shelf of the bookcase. I had forgotten that there was a low-ceilinged attic in the house, not much more than a tall crawl space. A small set of stairs led to it, near the top of the main staircase going up to the second floor. In this attic room, my grandparents had stored the hats, feather boas and assorted costumes they'd used in their amateur theatrics. I had loved to play among these treasures.

Standing on the first floor at the foot of the stairs, I remembered something that made me laugh out loud. In 1932, when I was four, family friends of the Pollard's had come to spend the afternoon. The family had twin girls who were my age. I told the girls about the costumes and they agreed to go and see them. While up in the attic, somehow, our sun suits had come off. Parents dressed their young kids in sun suits in those days. These were sleeveless, legless, one-piece affairs, suitable for children of either gender. I looked up at the attic door and couldn't recall whether I had talked the twins into disrobing or they had convinced me to do so. In any event, there we'd stood, three little nudes among the feather boas and hats, gazing at one another's *things* and marveling at the difference in them.

Suddenly grandmother Pollard's voice had called from the bottom of the stairs, two flights below.

"Dallas. Are you up there? What are you doing? Are the girls with you?" Panic reigned in the attic, a desperate attempt to get legs into leg holes and arms through arm holes.

"Dallas!" Again, my grandmother's voice.

"Yes, grandma, we're coming." It was not often that I had been able to get a laugh out of Katherine Pollard. My grandfather loved my youthful attempts at humor but grandma was a tough nut to crack. The attic door opened and the twins and I appeared and began clambering down the steps. Katherine glanced at the girls and a smile appeared on her face. I looked over at his playmates and discovered the cause of this anomaly: the sun suit on one of the twins was inside-out.

My grandfather and I took long walks together during the three days I stayed in Hartland. He pressed me for news about my life and about how my career was coming. One afternoon we returned from a trek through the brambles and boggy banks of Lull Brook. As we entered the kitchen Katherine's jaw dropped. "Look at your glasses, Dallas," she snapped. "They're caked with mud." She pulled her husband's spectacles off, polished them and positioned them back on his nose. Grandpa Pollard regarded his wife through his newly clean glasses and did a take.

"Why you're beautiful," he cried. "Give us a kiss!"

On the last day of my stay, I took a stroll to the Howe family home. I hadn't known it but Mrs. Howe was now running the general store in town. Avery, it seemed, had moved out, but one of his brothers got on the phone and in no time Avery arrived at the homestead in his pick-up. He was a good looking young man now. Both he and I were twenty. We reminisced and laughed for a bit. Then Avery took off in his truck to fetch his girlfriend at her job in the mill. I walked home. Grandmother fixed fried chicken for dinner, preparing extra for me to take on my trip home. The next morning Grandpa walked me down to the bus stop. I popped in to the store and said hello to Mrs. Howe. She had heard that I was still "putting on shows." I promised not to steal her boy away and make him a star. The bus came. I shook my grandfather's hand and boarded it. I had no way of knowing it then, but I was to have another twenty five years of loving connection with the old man, who lived in fine health to the ripe old age of ninety eight.

XII

Rocco Paladino and Irv Chipman, an Italian and a Jew, were, according to the Boston Globe, "reputed to have underworld connections." Rocky and Chippy, as they were known to their associates, took over the management of a Boston nightclub called the Mayfair. The club had flourished during the war as a second tier version of the Latin Quarter, which was run by a heavy hitter named Lou Walters (Barbara Walters father). The club had fallen on hard times after V J Day and had closed down. Meanwhile, up in Manhattan, in the east village, acquaintances of Rocky and Chippy were operating a transvestite joint called the Club 82. It featured female impersonators and was apparently making money hand over fist.

There had never been an attraction like that in staid old Boston. I remembered that when I was a kid, any man dressed as a woman in public would have been arrested on sight. Only on Halloween could drag queens legally walk the streets in their full regalia. They inaugurated what they called Artists and Models Balls, and pranced from ball to ball, teetering on their heels and smiling flirtatiously at the frustrated Irish cops. I was told that this is the reason that to this day there are big gay celebrations on Halloween.

1Rocky and Chippy decided that they would open a drag show at the old Mayfair Club. The under-the-table pay-offs must have been substantial, given the obvious objections the powerful Catholic Church would have been expected to make. They renamed the club The College Inn, and imported a slew of "queens" from the Club 82. A number of these moved into the Carlton House and the level of merriment there rose substantially. The show at the College Inn was part drag and part straight. The emcee was a straight comic named Bobby Ramsen, and there were novelty acts interspersed with flamboyant drag queen numbers. Perhaps this mixture was one of the ways that Rocky and Chippy managed to get permission to open.

I got a call from my manager, Fred Mack. The Ford Agency had called with an offer for me to play the place for two weeks at $90 per. I jumped at the chance. The joint was packed. Boston had never seen anything like it. Harvard and M.I.T. students came in droves. Some of them seem to have fallen in love. I would see them standing outside the rear entrance to the club, holding bouquets of flowers. Friends of Rocky and Chippy came too. "Made men" showed up with their women to enjoy the show and laugh at the drag queens. Rocky, the more gregarious of the two partners, held forth at his table in the bar, which was a separate room between the front entrance and the main club.

When I opened at the College Inn and did my hypnotism, Rocky Paladino stepped inside to take a look. He was fascinated. Night after night he watched. "This kid is really something," he told his cronies. "He can hypnotize anybody." The act seemed to appeal to his sense of power. He began inviting me to join his group in the outer room. Rocky's friends could not understand why the patrone was willing to allow a young comic with a crew cut to join them at their sanctum sanctorum.

I found my boss' friends endlessly fascinating. They were not educated in any traditional way, but had, with only a few exceptions, real street smarts. Power radiated off of them, and because of this they attracted the most beautiful of women. Going back to the cave days, I realized, the Alpha male had gotten the female with the least fur. In addition to being beautiful, the women at Rocky's table were brainy; no bimbos need apply.

"Beans," Rocky would call out as I walked past his table. "Oscar! Sit down. Take a load off!" Rocky called me Oscar Beans; I didn't know why. To my delight, my engagement at the College Inn was extended and I was given a raise. I had my own little dressing room back stage. The cute young transvestites flirted with me. One of them would knock on my door as show time approached. "Five minutes, Miss Bean!" he'd call.

In Washington, D.C. the Kefauver hearings into organized crime became the first news event to be nationally televised. Rocky was subpoenaed. A TV was set up in the outer bar and I came by on the day when Rocky was scheduled to testify.

"Mr. Paladino," Senator Kefauver asked. "On or about the fifth of October in nineteen and forty seven, did you or did you not..."

"Senator, I respectfully decline to answer on the basis of my fifth amendment rights." Rocky was a celebrity now. A party was thrown for him in the outer room on the night he returned from the capitol, and I was invited.

"Sit down, Oscar." Rocky made a place next to him at the table. "So how's it hangin' ? Anyone bothering you, giving you a hard time, you let me know and I'll have him taken care of. Capeesh?" I promised that I would do so. One of "the boys" at the table began telling a story about Frank Costello, head of the New York crime syndicate, and an apparent friend of Rocky's. I had had a beer or two. I turned to my boss and asked, "Is Costello really a killer, Rocky?" A silence fell over the table. I had committed a terrible gaffe. But Rocky was endlessly forgiving to his young protégée.

"Beans," he said. "Costello is no more of a killer than…" I could see that his lips were about to form the words, "I am," He couldn't bring himself to say it. "*You* are," he finished the sentence.

One evening when I was in the process of selecting the three volunteers for my act, a fourth one, unbidden, joined them. When I whispered to the guy to "play along," a sneer came over his face and he returned to his seat. Unbeknownst to me, the interloper was an associate of Rocky's by the name of Angie. He was from a famiglia in Winthrop. At Rocky's table in the outer bar area before the show, Angie had listened to Rocky brag about this kid who could hypnotize anybody.

"A C-note says he can't do me."

"You're on," Rocky had replied. After the performance a waiter came to my dressing room.

"Rocky wants to see you in the office." I was trembling. I knocked on the office door.

"Come in, Oscar," Rocky called. I entered the office.

"What Angie tells me, Beans. Say it isn't so." I shuffled my feet and looked down at the floor.

"Well," I began. Rockys eyes turned as cold as ice.

"Get out," he said. I left. I didn't even bother to collect my pay. I went home to the Carleton House and packed my things. The next day I took a Greyhound bus to Philadelphia.

XIII

I had two hundred dollars saved up to go to Philly (better than Ben Franklin had done). I didn't know a living soul there. It was early June. I had heard the name of a talent agency and had written down the address of a hotel on Spruce Street where variety performers were known to stay. Ruthie had had a fling with Bobby Ramsen, the comic at the College Inn, so I only made a perfunctory goodbye phone call to her. I told George that I'd stay in touch and telephoned Isobel Hickey to say goodbye. When I checked into the hotel in Philly, I wrote to Parker to tell him where I was and what had happened.

I had selected Philadelphia to move to because, as was the case in Boston, there was a full year of work booked out of that city: gigs like the Moose Club in Altoona and the V. F.W. hall in Harrisburg, as well as better jobs. I could have stayed in Boston and continued to work; I wasn't really afraid that Rocky would take a contract out on me. I felt genuinely bad about the patrone; I had come to like him and I knew that the feeling had been reciprocated. (Years later, when I was starring on Broadway and a regular on the Ed Sullivan Show, Rocky and I ran into each other at the Latin Quarter in New York City. I had gone there to see Milton Berle. "Oscar," Rocky cried, and jumped up from his table to give me a hug. "You owe it all to me. If it wasn't for me you'd still be working in Boston!"

What had happened at the College Inn that night had been the catalyst for something that I had pretty much decided on anyway. It was time to let go of the magic and hypnotism and start doing straight stand-up comedy. Known as I was in Boston, this would have been impossible. I needed a new locale to make a fresh start. I had written almost enough original comedy to flesh out an act. But not quite enough, so I "borrowed" a routine from the great comedian, Victor Borge, who had recorded an album. I rationalized that this was a benign sort of theft because Borge would never work the Moose Club, and no one there would ever have heard of Victor Borge. I planned on using this routine ("phonetic punctuation") only until I had come up with enough of my own material to make up for the loss of the hypnotism.

The first morning when I awoke in his hotel room in Philadelphia, I headed for the booking agency. The secretary told me to leave a picture. I asked if I could speak to one of the agents. I was told they were busy and that since I had never worked anywhere in town anyway there was no point in my waiting around, they wouldn't be able to send me out on a job.

Not knowing what else to do, I sat in the outer waiting room. A couple of performers came in. I asked them for the names of other agents, which they gave me. I went to those agencies and received a comparably cold reception. I had passed an Automat restaurant, the first one I had ever seen, and went there for lunch. Not knowing if or when I might earn any more money I had limited myself to a budget of twenty five cents for lunch and the same for dinner. Most items at the Automat cost a nickel. I walked past the steam table, checking out what was being offered there, or in the small coin-operated cubicles.

Making my decision, I selected two orders of home fries and a side of spinach. This nearly filled the plate. I then inserted a nickel into the coin slot next to a little window, behind which sat a pair of rolls with butter. I had now spent twenty cents, leaving me with a nickel for dessert. I moved to the iced tea spigot, beside which was a bowl heaped with lemon wedges. Helping myself to half a dozen of these, I squeezed them into a glass of (free) ice water. There was a sugar bowl on each table. In this way, I was able to enjoy a delicious lemonade for nothing. The meal was quite filling. I had become a monetary vegetarian. I inspected the dessert choices and purchased a slice of jellyroll with my last nickel. I walked out of the restaurant feeling satisfied.

After lunch, I headed for a drugstore. In those days, twenty five cent books (which is what paperbacks cost and were called) got displayed on wire racks in pharmacies. I chose a biography of Marie Curie. I was starting to experience a hunger for knowledge, which I had denied myself for all my years in school. Limited budget or not, I doled out a precious quarter of a dollar every day for a non-fiction book. My subjects of choice included philosophy, history and astronomy. I devoured stories of the great inventers and explorers. For some reason, it never occurred to me to find a library. Each day I made the rounds of booking agents, got rejected, bought another paperback book and retreated to my hole on Spruce Street to read it. My room at the hotel was tiny. It shared a bathroom with the adjacent room. The door to that room had to be locked when I was using the facilities and then unlocked when I was through.

Three weeks went by. No agents would see me. My savings were nearly gone and I was starting to despair. I wrote regularly to Parker, who saved the letters he received. Years later he returned some of them to me. I had written the following letter to him at that time:

Sun. aft. June 25, 1950
Philly

Yo Parker. Hope all's well. It's hot as hell here in the City of Brotherly Love. I came at an importune time of year, just as a lot of clubs were closing down for the summer. And I spent hours waiting in agents' offices only to get the fluff. Finally, I said "To hell with this" (yes I did) and decided to pick out a club and try to book myself into it. So I went to a place called Marty Bohn's Nut Club and asked if I could go on for free. They let me and I did well and they said they could use me. But as luck would have it, the following week was their last full week until the fall and that was already booked. But for some reason there were three days available after that week at the very end of the season. (Are you following this?) They knew I was over a barrel so they offered me $15 a night. Well beggars can't be choosers so I said OK. I figured it was an in-town club and maybe I could get some agents to come and catch me.

Anyway I did the job and no agents came at all. So I was about ready to throw in the towel and give up, but a guy I didn't know named Tommy Tattler called at the hotel. He was some kind of a manager. He said he'd heard about me through another act at the Nut Club and would I come and do a freebee at a place called Phillip's so he could see me. I said OK and that night (this was last Thursday) I did the show and it went great. (I didn't do any magic or hypnotism, by the way, just talk). So, I got a contract to play there for two weeks for $100 a week and this guy Tommy Tattler is going to handle me from now on, so with any luck at all my troubles will be over. Do you hear anything from Ruthie? Is she still up to no good with Bobby Ramsen? Damn. Please give my love to Claire. Miss you, buddy. Any new tricks up your sleeve?

Orson.

Out of nowhere, things began to turn around. In addition to work, I started to make some friends. A comic named Joey Karter followed me from club to club, watching my act and laughing. We began hanging out at a late night restaurant called the Harvey House. It was on Broad Street near the Shubert Theater. Comics congregated there after their late shows.

Tommy Tattler was an odd duck, a funny little guy with white hair and a pencil moustache. But he started to get me jobs: The Peacock Café in Andalusia, The Bridge in Johnstown, the Veterans of Foreign Wars hall in Lewistown. In each of these towns, I would check into a fleabag hotel by the bus station. I would write new material during the day and try it out at night in the club. Odd routines were coming to me: an Australian who falls in love with an ostrich; a fan obsessed with Bela Lugosi; a Martian who buys his son a pet goo-goo (which then eats his landlady's kid).

I got booked into a club called the Crossroads. It was in Maryland, but on the border of the District of Columbia. The star of the show was a stripper named Pat "Amber" Holliday. No exotic dancers were allowed in the nation's capitol, so residents of the District who were fans of that art form had to take the short drive to the state line. Amber was extraordinary. Her toned body was oiled and sinewy. She wore leopard skin briefs and writhed on stage to the sound of jungle drums. She packed the house. I was emcee of the show. One night there was a table of men whom I recognized as CBS news people. Walter Cronkite was there, along with Eric Severeid. Amber finished her dance by taking off her bra. She stood there for a moment in all her glory and then the lights went out. When they came back on, I was at the microphone with my mouth hanging open. I said, "Good heavens!" The CBS guys howled. Then I said, "I haven't seen anything like that since I was weaned!" The newsmen applauded. They invited me over to their table. Years later, I ran into Cronkite, who said to me, "Do you remember where we first met?" Some thrill to be remembered by the most trusted man in America.

I returned to Philly. As I left the bus station and headed to my hotel, a comic I knew slightly from the Harvey House approached me.

"Hey Bean," he said. "You think Joey Karter is your friend? The guy stole your Victor Borge routine!" I realized that it was time to move on. I had worked what there was to be had in and around Philly. My act was all original material now and I knew that I should bring it to New York. I said goodbye to Tommy Tattler and thanked him. I splurged and took the train to Manhattan, rather than riding the Greyhound. I checked into the Capitol Hotel on Eighth Avenue, across from the old Madison Square Garden. Billy Graham was doing his Christian Crusade there. His name was on the marquee. I thought of a gag line: Wrestling Tonight! Billy Graham VS the Devil! The elevator operator (there were still elevator operators in those days) had a bad haircut and a boil on the back of his neck. He let out two big sighs as he carried me up to my room on the thirteenth floor. When he opened the elevator door, he turned to me with misty eyes, let out another sigh and said, "I dunno." He looked at me for a moment and then added, " Ya know?" I nodded that I did.

As had been the case in Philadelphia, I knew no-one in New York. I was starting from scratch all over again. No agent, no manager, no connections but like the bumblebee who doesn't know he can't fly, I was filled with a brio born of ignorance. I had heard of a supper club called The Blue Angel. Sophisticated chanteuses played there. It was one of the most famous boites in the country. The club was on East 55th Street. I decided that I would just pop in and see what happened. I sauntered across town in the middle of the afternoon, passing Times Square, Sixth Avenue, Fifth, Madison and Park. The Blue Angel was housed in a brownstone between Lexington and Third. I tried the front door and found it unlocked. I walked in. Nobody was around. The place was dimly lit and empty. There was a bar on the left and a hatcheck stand on the right, Tables and booths filled the room. A grand piano was in the corner. I saw a pair of swinging doors ahead of me, pushed them open and took a look inside. The main room was a long slender space with tiny tables and a little stage at the rear.

A flight of steps between the piano and the hatcheck booth led upstairs. I climbed them. Men's and women's restrooms were in the upper hall. A light shown from an open door at the end of the corridor. I approached it. A middle aged man was sitting at a desk, counting a pile of receipts. He looked up as I poked my head in the door.

"What do you want?" he asked.

"I'm a comic." The man stared at me, taking in my crew cut and the suit I was wearing.

"Say something funny."

"Belly button."

There was a long pause. The man looked at me. A faint smile came over his face. Then he said, "I'm short an act tonight. Come by at ten and I'll put you on and have a look."

The man at the desk was Max Gordon, the proprietor. I took a cab back across town to my hotel. I went over my routines, selecting the best ones. I was strangely calm. I took the elevator down and walked to a tailor shop I had spotted on 50th and Seventh. A sign in the window said that for thirty five cents the proprietor would "sponge and press" a suit. There was a little cubicle where the client could undress and wait. When the job was done the tailor handed me the suit and I put it on, paid for the job and walked back to my hotel. In my room I hung up the suit and removed a clean shirt from my suitcase. I had a copy of the New York Herald Tribune ready for making my paper tree. I had purchased the Tribune rather than the Times because I thought the name was funnier. I lay down to rest, going over my act for one last time.

At eight thirty, I got dressed and left the hotel. I took the 50th Street, cross-town bus to Lexington Ave. I walked the five blocks north to 55th Street and turned right toward Third Avenue to get to the Blue Angel. I went in. The joint was jumping. I sat down at the bar, ordered a Coke, and in a little while Max Gordon appeared.

"Oh, hello there," he said. "Why don't you go stand in the back and get a feel of the room." I followed him through the swinging doors and into the main room. I leaned against the rear wall and watched. A singer named Anita Ellis was on. She was very good. The audience applauded after each number. When my turn came, the emcee announced that an extra added attraction would be next. There was a smattering of polite applause and, holding my copy of the Herald Tribune, I walked up the aisle and stood behind the microphone.

"Good evening," I said, "My name is Orson Bean. Harvard 48 (pause) Yale nothing." The audience laughed. They looked at my crew cut and grey flannel suit. I did not look like any comedian they had ever seen. "All my people are from New England," I told them. "My grandfather used to warn me against southerners. He'd say, 'Stay away from Hartford.'" I recounted the tale of my famous ancestor Ezekiel Bean, the proprietor of a tavern in Boston during the American Revolution. Ezekiel Bean "*poured* the shot heard 'round the world.'" The audience laughed. I did a mock broadcast of the riot that broke out between the teams at the annual Harvard-Yale football game: "Fists are flying. Blood has been spilt. The field is stained a vivid blue!" I did my goo-goo routine, and closed by making the paper Eucalyptus tree and delivering my faux lecture on the Roman Empire. The audience went nuts. I had never gotten such laughs in my life. My head was reeling.

Max Gordon spoke to me after the show and signed me on the spot to a six months contract. I was to begin the next night. An associate of the powerful syndicated columnist Walter Winchell had been in the house. The publicist for the club told me to look in the Daily Mirror the next day. I returned to my room at the hotel and tried to sleep. I thought about the Portuguese guy who had cancelled me on Christmas Eve. In the morning, Winchell's column appeared. It said: "His name is Orson Bean. We never heard of him either. He went on unannounced at the Blue Angel last night and got big laughs. The audience applauded for four bows." Winchell was the most important columnist in America. Two days later a second item appeared: "Orson Bean clicked at the Blue Angel. Due to the mention in our column, the place was packed."

My career was off and running.

XIV

With a contract for six months at $125 a week in my pocket, I set about finding a place to live: a small apartment on Third Avenue and 38th Street. Signing a lease for $82.50 a month was traumatic, but I did it. I bought some new clothes so I wouldn't have to take my one suit to the "sponge and press" tailor. The hatcheck girl at the Blue Angel took me under her wing and suggested that I go see a shrink she knew. I visited him three times a week for ten years, trying to figure out why, when everything finally seemed to be going my way, I was less than euphoric.

I became more or less house comic at the club and played there six months out of the year for almost as long as I went to the shrink. The club was "in." Celebrities came every night. Bob Hope watched the show, then graciously asked me to join him at his table. Bob Hope, my childhood idol, whom Parker and I had worshipped at the Boston Garden! The gorgeous movie star Esther Williams came, and I was asked to sit with her and have a picture taken. I flashed on a Burlesque show I'd sneaked into in my youth. The comic is arrested and told that anything he says may be held against him. "Esther Williams!" he cries.

Orson Welles appeared one night. He ordered me to his table, scowled and muttered, "You stole my name." Brendan Behan showed up. His play, *The Hostage*, was on Broadway. He invited me to join him after the late performance. Then he suggested we find a different bar where we could talk. My ego soared. The great Brendan Behan wanting to talk with me. At the other bar he picked up another person, then a third and fourth. He couldn't stand to be alone with his demons.

I decided I needed to learn how to act and enrolled in theater classes. I studied for years with all the well-known teachers (Uta Hagen, Eli Wallach, Wynn Handman). I studied singing and tap dancing, too. No mime.

An agent came into the Blue Angel, saw my act and booked me into, of all things, the Palace Theater. In 1950 Judy Garland had done her one-woman show there, which she famously ended by sitting on the front edge of the stage with her feet dangling in the orchestra pit, and singing Somewhere Over the Rainbow. She did her show twice a day, and it brought back vaudeville! Suddenly (for a few years) variety performers who had been eking out an existence at State Fairs, hoping for a shot on the Ed Sullivan Show, found work.

Heading the bill at the Palace were Buck and Bubbles, a pair of stars from old Black Broadway reviews like Bubblin' Brown Sugar. Buck, tall and handsome, a great tap dancer, Bubbles, short, stout and funny. I watched every show to learn what I could from their prodigious skill. Fourth on the bill was a guy with a trained crow. Astonishingly, the bird perched on his arm and whistled and sang, ending the act with a patriotic melody. It wasn't until the second day that I realized the crow was a fake. The guy, a ventriloquist, wore a false arm, which the faux crow sat on. His real arm was up inside the bird, operating it with continuous, subtle movements that made it look uncannily alive.

Also in the show was an act I had seen as a kid at the RKO Theater in Boston: Lowe, Hite and Stanley. Lowe was a dwarf, Hite was a giant, and Stanley was normal sized. They did eight minutes of comic tumbling, ending with Lowe's huge hand thumbing Hite's tiny nose. Corn-ball but funny. The giant turned out to be an intellectual who tried to discuss Schopenhauer with me. I listened politely, but couldn't understand him.

When I wasn't at the club in New York, I worked from time to time at vaudeville theaters around the country where I appeared with such acts as Fink's Mules, LeFarge's Cockatoos, and Gautier's Dogs and Monkeys. At a theater in Pennsylvania I was on the bill once again with Lowe, Hite and Stanley. There was a different Stanley in the act by then. The giant and the dwarf weren't going to pay a regular-sized guy anything, so they kept replacing him. This time, the giant tried to discuss Goethe.

Back at the Blue Angel, Broadway producers came to the club and started to cast me in plays, so I could put my acting lessons to work. The first one, a comedy called Josephine based on F. Scott Fitzgerald stories, closed during its out-of-town tryout, never making it in to the *Great White Way*. But Variety reviewed it in Wilmington and said, "Orson Bean steals every scene in which he appears." The second one, *Men of Distinction*, written by Richard Condon, who shortly after that wrote *The Manchurian Candidate*, did get to Broadway. It got rough reviews and closed in three days. But Walter Kerr, the critic for the Herald-Tribune, wrote, "As is usually the case with this sort of disaster, a couple of performers crawl cheerfully out of the wreckage. One of these is Orson Bean..."

I began to be cast in TV dramas. In those days, everything was live. There was no room to make a mistake. If you did goof up, you covered it as best you could. In one show, an actress grabbed a baby from its crib, ran out of the room and down a flight of stairs. Live on the air, she dropped the baby, then picked it up and continued to run out of the house. The network was so deluged with phone calls that they had to stop the program and explain that, as the actress passed briefly out of the bedroom door and was not seen for an instant, the live baby was switched for a doll wrapped in a similar blanket and it was the doll that had fallen.

William F. Buckley saw me at the Blue Angel and invited me to speak to an audience of his intellectual friends at The Yale Club. I did my American Revolution stuff and got howls. I was hob-knobbing with the great and the near great, putting on a swell front ...but feeling completely out of it. I felt like I was walking in a dream.

CBS Television decided to produce a variety show called *The Blue Angel* and hired me to host it. They built sets to look like the outer area with its bar and hat-check booth, and the main room with its stage. I did comedy monologues and introduced the guest performers, sophisticated entertainers like Hildegard and Pearl Bailey. The show was aired from CBS Studio 50 on 53rd and Broadway (where David Letterman broadcasts now). The CBS censors back then were ruthless. I would sit on a stool and read gossip items from the newspaper: "Will Debbie say 'yes' to Eddie Fisher?" I look up from the paper. "Depends on what the question is!" Censored. Too racy. "Ezekiel Bean *poured* the shot heard 'round the world." Censored. No mention of alcohol allowed. Compare that to the language on TV today. (And I walked through four foot drifts of snow to deliver my jokes.)

———•·•———

But, of course, the whole culture has changed, like it or not and for better or for worse. The fifties are made fun of; New York in the fifties was great for me. The streets were safe; couple strolled down 52nd Street at 2 AM, heading for the jazz joints. There was a drugstore open every few blocks. The subways ran all night and cost a nickel. If you thought you were going to miss a train, you didn't bother to hurry because another one would be along in a few minutes.

Alright, enough codger talk; it wasn't all wonderful. When Pearl Bailey and other Black performers appeared on The Blue Angel show, I was warned not to touch them. Any physical contact between a white person and a Black one on the tube would cause stations in the south to cut away. That's the way it was. The network kept The Blue Angel Show on for twenty six weeks, then decided the concept was too hip for the country.

———•·•———

I finally made it into a hit show on Broadway, John Murray Anderson's Almanac, the last of the great "feathers and boobs" musical revues. It was 1953 and I was twenty five years old. The show had a pre-Broadway try out in

Boston at the Shubert Theater, so my father could come and see it. So could Parker. In New York it was booked into the Imperial Theater, a beautiful, old musical house on 45th Street. Hermione Gingold, a British comedienne, was the star. I sang a song called The Merry Little Minuet, about the woes that beset the human race. It was written by Sheldon Harnick, who later became famous for Fiddler on the Roof. I did monologues and built my paper tree. On opening night, the audience ate it up.

Back then, there was an all-night news stand at the corner of Broadway and 42nd Street, where theater people were able to get the bull-dog editions of the New York Times and the other morning papers (there were seven dailies back then—The Times, Herald-Tribune. News, Mirror, Post, World-Telegram and Journal-American). Everybody wanted to be first to see whether a show was going to be a hit. The papers arrived at 11:30, when a truck pulled up and a bundle was tossed onto the sidewalk. The news stand operator would snip off the wire which held the stack of papers together, and a cast of characters out of Damon Runyan would reach for copies. There were publicists and flacks, producers, performers, insomniacs and assorted other night creatures.

I was dating the hat-check girl from the Blue Angel. She came to my opening in Almanac and waited with me at the news stand to see what the critic for the Times would have to say. His name was Brooks Atkinson and he was the dean of American theater reviewers, erudite and polished, tough when he had to be, but without the streak of meanness which characterizes a lot of critics today. Atkinson loved the show, praising the stars, Hermione Gingold and Billy DeWolfe. He also had kind words for me, saying that my material was "concise and convulsing." To celebrate, the hat-check girl and I ate a tube steak in the all night hot dog emporium next to the news stand.

———•———

In 1953, 42nd Street was very different from the garish, drug-ridden environment it was later to become. The New Amsterdam, a gorgeous old musical theater (much later beautifully restored by the Disney organization) had become a threadbare but clean picture house. Families could enjoy second-run movies there—a quarter for adults, fifteen cents for kids. Down the block was the Laff Movie which featured revivals of Laurel and Hardy and Harold Lloyd flicks. It had fun-house mirrors on its façade. Tourists would stand with their kids on the sidewalk and giggle at their distorted images.

Next to the Laff Movie was Hubert's Flea Circus and Museum of Oddities. For a quarter you could see an old-fashioned freak show. One of the attractions was my old favorite, Albert-Alberta, the half-man, half-woman. Albert's right leg was strong and hairy, and he wore a work boot on it. The other was smooth and silky and sported a pump. One arm was muscular, the other quite feminine. He had a voluptuous breast on his left side of his chest; the other side was flat and hirsute. His hair was cut short on the right, and long and coifed on the left. I spoke to Albert, introduced myself, and said that I had seen him in my youth at Revere Beach in Boston.

"Show business isn't what it used to be," said Albert. But he was clearly pleased to have a fan from the old days.

For an extra quarter, visitors to the museum could watch the entrepreneur, Hubert, present his flea circus. Of course, I had to take this in. In a small room off the main hall fifteen or so audience members would gather around a tall stand with a little stage on it. Hubert would perch on a box behind the podium. Each of us was handed a magnifying glass with a handle on it, the better to see the stars of the show. One by one, the performers appeared. A flea lay on his back, balancing a tiny ball. As he moved his legs, the ball spun. Then Hubert nudged the flea with a tooth pick and it kicked the ball onto the feet of a flea next to it, where it continued to spin. I was dumb-founded. Other cast members contributed an exhibition of flea wrestling.

The show concluded with a chariot race—half a dozen fleas hooked up to tiny tumbrels ran across the felt covered stage, accompanied by Hubert's instructive patter. "You may wager on the outcome if you like, ladies and gentlemen, but no coin of the realm is to change hands, please; my fleas are deeply moral." After the show Hubert rolled up his sleeve and those who cared were able to watch as he rewarded each of his actors with a bit of blood from his forearm.

John Murray Anderson's Almanac ran for a year. A gorgeous, young Harry Belafonte was in the show, and backstage, beautiful chorines fought for his affections. I saw two of them get into a hair-pulling, screaming, wrestling match on the floor outside his dressing room. Life Magazine did a story on the show and chose to print a full-page picture of me with my paper tree. I won the Theater World Award for my performance. I was becoming famous. I should have been on top of the world, but I wasn't. I would go to my shrink, lie on his couch, and tell him that life was "just OK." There was a hole in me that just never got filled.

———◆——

Back in New York, Ed Sullivan (who had seen me in the Broadway review) booked me on his show. I appeared seven times. People started to recognize me in the street. It was heady.

———◆——

In the spring of '55, I got an offer to star in a Broadway play called *Will Success Spoil Rock Hunter*. It would go into rehearsal in the fall, so I decided, having a bit of dough saved up, that I would take a vacation. I rented a cottage on Fire Island for the month of July. It was my first such indulgence. I had taken not so much as a day off since arriving in New York, much less spent any extravagant money on myself. Fire Island is a spit of land along the south shore of Long Island. It has several "towns," which usually consist of a store around which houses cluster. Ocean Beach was the town I selected to rent in, because I knew that Mel Brooks, the funniest man in the world, owned a house there. Just being near him, I figured, some funny might rub off on me.

The town had a sea breeze, a white sandy beach, and was only a couple of hours away from the city, the last forty minutes of which was a ferry ride from the mainland. A restaurant sat on either side of the dock at which the ferry arrived in Ocean Beach, and one of them had a jumping bar.

I found a little place to rent half way between the beach and the town (the two restaurants, a grocery store, an ice cream parlor and a sort of civic center where they showed 16 mm movies every evening). Kids ran wild in Ocean Beach. No motor vehicles drove on Fire Island, so their parents knew they would be safe.

I walked past Mel Brooks' house one day. Mel was sitting on his porch with his friend, Carl Reiner. I slowed down and said Hi, hoping they might recognize me and invite me to stop. They did. It was one of the great afternoons of my life. The two comics were cracking each other up, working on a routine they were developing called The Second Man. The second man was the same little guy who later emerged as The Two Thousand Year Old Man. But in this earlier version, he was the assistant to famous historical characters—a sail-maker to Blackbeard the Pirate, a stone cutter to Moses. ("I chiseled out fifteen commandments on three tablets for him. A thoughtless person, he was, and clumsy. So, suddenly, it's *ten* commandments! And he didn't even tell me sorry."

I spent the days basking on the beach and the evenings at the bar. I was starting to be recognized, hoping to meet some girls. I did meet a few, nothing much. One day as I was walking to the store, a voice called out my name. I turned and saw a man I recognized. It was John Henry Faulk. I had run into him on Madison Avenue, a likeable guy who did a daily afternoon radio show on the local CBS affiliate in New York, and spent weekends at his cottage in Ocean Park.

"C'mon over to my place tonight, kid. I think you'll find it interesting." Johnny Falk was a Texan of inordinate charm. He had an easy-going way about him and a drawl which made him sound all-American. Faulk was well known on Fire Island; he had a good looking wife, three tow-headed kids, and a pet goat. The goat would come when he called, follow him down the sidewalk, and do everything but carry home the paper. John told wonderful stories on his radio show about the poor people of Texas. He'd do them in dialect, and there was one about a little girl who dreamed of someday owning a pair of shoes, which had left me in tears when I heard it.

I showed up that night at the address Faulk had given me, and was surprised to see a bunch of recognizable faces. Mrs. Faulk served drinks, the tanned and happy children clamored to stay up longer, the goat ran in and out of the house, and the guests talked politics.

In the summer of '55 the communications industry was in the grips of a blacklist. A book called Red Channels had been published, naming the actors, directors and writers its editors thought might be Communists, and the people on the list were finding it hard to get work. Every few weeks, Red Channels put out a news bulletin called Counterattack, which added more names. A super-patriot grocer from Syracuse had started writing to the big food companies like Heinz and Campbell's, telling them they need no longer send him their cans of soup to sell if they sponsored TV programs featuring any of the actors listed in Red Channels or Counter Attack.

The television and radio performers' union (AFTRA) was ripped apart over the issue of blacklisting. For years in movies and radio, back in the forties, a group of left wing producers and directors had hired nothing but fellow left-wing actors. This in turn had created a hard-core bunch of bitter conservative (sometimes, reactionary) actors who were burning for revenge by the time the McCarthy red scare hysteria hit the industry.

Things were so badly split that when performers came to union meetings, they'd sit on the right or left side of the hall to show their political leanings. Conservatives controlled the board of directors, the left wing packed meetings (and hooted at the board) and the rest of the membership was scared or apathetic. As a result, the union took no stand on blacklisting, thus in effect, supporting it.

The summer of '55 was a hot one, both meteorologically and politically. In Maine, agents of the federal government entered the estate of an accused Communist, the brilliant and eccentric psychiatrist Wilhelm Reich. Using sledge hammers, they smashed his so-called Orgone boxes. In New York, other agents of the government shoveled piles of his books into furnaces in the city incinerator in downtown Manhattan. This took place 25 years after the Nazi book burning in Berlin.

At Johnny Faulk's house on Fire Island, the blacklist became the topic of conversation on weekend evenings. The Hollywood Ten had been driven out of the movies, and big stars and well-known supporting players were washed up in the business. Even Lucille Ball made headlines when someone dug up the fact that she'd once voted for a Communist candidate for Congress. Desi Arnez came to the rescue by calling a press conference to deny his wife was a Red.

"You know Lucy," he said. "She didn't even know who the hell she was voting for." So, the smartest business woman in Hollywood saved herself by acting like the dizzy dame she played on her series. One week that summer, the Un-American Activities Committee came to New York and subpoenaed a bunch of actors it said were Reds, Pinkos or dupes. A protest meeting was called at Carnegie Hall, and I, the do-gooder, took a ferry in to appear at it. While I was waiting backstage to go on, a left-wing friend spotted me. "What the hell are you doing here?" he said. "The place is lousy with FBI agents, taking everybody's name down." Undeterred, I went on and told some jokes.

———·◦·———

Night after night on Fire Island, John Henry Faulk held forth on the evils of the blacklist. People within the union were cooperating with Counter Attack to "rid the airwaves of Reds."

"Honey," Johnny would say in his charming Texas drawl, "don't kid yourself. These people are fascists and dangerous. They'll sit there grinnin' like egg-sucking dogs, all friendly-like, but they'll kill us and they'll kill the country."

Galvanized, a group of performers decided to form a slate of candidates and run for union office. Maybe we could destroy the blacklist. We'd call ourselves The Middle-of-the-Road Slate and be politically neither left nor right. Word of the plan spread through the industry. Jack Paar joined the slate. So did Tony Randall and the respected CBS news man, Charles Collingwood. I was excited as hell.

It was now August. The group gathered at Johnny Faulk's Manhattan apartment to finalize our plans. When the meeting was called to order, somebody said, "You know, we've really got to offer the membership a clean slate. We shouldn't be running any of the tired old faces who've been involved in left-wing politics, and I hate to say it, but a few of us have been." There was an embarrassed pause, and then a fairly well-known actor spoke up.

"Well, I guess that's my cue to bow out. It would have been fun, and I'd like to go along for the ride, but I have been a joiner in my day, and I agree that the slate should be completely clean." There were a few dissenting cries but reason prevailed and his name was regretfully withdrawn. One other performer said that he too had better back off, and then I opened my mouth to confess my appearance at Carnegie Hall. Someone asked if there was anything else?

"No, except I voted for Adlai Stevenson." There was laughter all around and Johnny said, "Hell, honey. You're as pure as a Baptist preacher's six year old daughter. They can't get you for that one little thing. Stick with us, honey."

The New York Times wrote about the slate and when the election was held, the Middle-of-the-Roaders won a smashing victory. Charles Collingwood became president of the New York local of AFTRA, I became first vice president, and Johnny Faulk was elected second veep. The Times and everyone else agreed that the blacklist had been dealt a serious blow.

A few weeks later my phone rang. I recognized the voice right away. It was Ed Sullivan. I was booked to be on his show the following Sunday and I figured he was calling to discuss the material I'd do.

"Orson," said Ed, "have you heard about Counterattack?" I could feel the blood draining out of my face. "They've cited you in today's issue and I'm afraid Sunday's booking is out. In fact, I won't be able to use you at all anymore." I felt sick. "If you tell anyone I called," Ed went on, "I'll have to deny it."

"I understand. Can you say what they wrote about me?"

"Sure. They say you appeared at some Communist meeting and did a skit ridiculing the Un-American Activities group."

"I did one of the dumb routines I've done on your show."

"Well," said Ed Sullivan, "I'll help when I can." He hung up.

I sat thunderstruck. How could they have nailed me for that one appearance? How could they say I was a Communist or a Communist dupe or a Communist sympathizer because of that one protest meeting?

I pulled myself together and started frantically making phone calls.

Charles Collingwood was in trouble too. Counterattack had condemned him for writing a critical letter to the House Un-American Activities Committee. CBS was meeting to decide what to do about him. Finally, I got a look at the news bulletin. It was a condemnation of the Middle-of-the-Road Slate, and it asked rhetorically just how middle of the road the candidates were. To answer the question, it listed the top three officers, Collingwood, Bean and Faulk. Starting with John Henry, it said, "How about Faulk? What is his public record? According to The Daily Worker of April 22, 1946..." I read with shock as it went on and on: Johnny at "Headline Cabaret, sponsored by Stage for Action, officially designated as a Communist Front. Johnny appearing with Paul Robeson (!) at the Communist Jefferson School; Johnny sending greetings to Peoples' Songs, a Red publication; Johnny as U.S. sponsor of the American Continental Congress for Peace in Mexico City; Johnny at Showtime for Wallace, staged by Progressive Citizens of America, a Communist front."

When the bulletin was finally through with Johnny, it turned to the other two officers on the slate. It said that I had appeared at the protest meeting and it mentioned Charlie's letter. By themselves, the charges against Collingwood and me would have been worth zip. Lumped in with all they had to say against Faulk, they added up to a grim picture. I was appalled. How could Counterattack have made up such stuff about Johnny? He was sure it couldn't be true or John wouldn't have jeopardized the whole slate by running.

I dashed up to Johnny's office at CBS. "It's not true, is it, John? You didn't appear at those places did you?"

"Aw, honey, what does it matter? Don't you see those people are fascists? If they didn't have something on us, they'd have made something up." I stood staring at Johnny. My ears were burning. I wanted to slug him. Instead, I walked out of his office and went home.

———

Overnight, my TV appearances dried up. I saw actors cross the street to avoid being seen talking to me. I was even snubbed by the doorman at CBS. Charles Collingwood held on by the skin of his teeth with the help of Edward R. Murrow and other news men. The network sent him to be a correspondent in London. Johnny Faulk was fired from his radio show and decided to sue AWARE and the grocer in Syracuse. He became the martyr of Madison Avenue. His friends raised money to support him. He became obsessed with his plans with the law suit. He thought and spoke of nothing else. His marriage came apart and his wife and kids left. I never found out what happened to the goat.

Faulk hired Louis Nizer, a famous and brilliant lawyer. The case was finally heard at the courthouse in lower Manhattan. While the trial was in progress, I went down to watch Nizer in action. He was astonishing. He made the black-listers look ridiculous. He made Johnny look like Jesus. I spoke to Faulk out in the hall and remarked on how Nizer had demolished the other side that morning.

"But was the other side telling the truth," I asked?

"The point is, they didn't *prove* it," said Johnny. "They were sloppy and they were bad detectives and we're gonna kill 'em." No wife, no kids, no job, no future and his eyes gleaming like Joan of Arc's.

Louis Nizer won the case for Johnny and the court awarded him a lot of money, but he didn't collect it because, in a Hollywood-style twist, the Syracuse grocer died while the jury was out deliberating, and AWARE was broke. He wrote a book about his experience but it didn't seem to sell too many copies. The last time I heard of him, he was back in Texas, traveling around and lecturing on man's inhumanity to man, as practiced by grocers in Syracuse.

Will Success Spoil Rock Hunter became a hit. (God was looking after me before I believed in Him. Or maybe it was a coincidence?) The blacklist never had much of an effect in the theater because there were no sponsors involved. It was Campbell's Soup which blacklisted actors and directors, not the viewing public or even the networks. For them, the blacklist was an expensive inconvenience. They had to pay Red Channels to "clear" actors. The fee was fifty bucks a head and had to be paid every week, even if the actor had been cleared the week before.

Will Success Spoil Rock Hunter ran a year, after which I booked a tour in summer stock. On Cape Cod near the Falmouth Playhouse, a fancy hotel invited actors from the theater to come and use their swimming pool. I gratefully accepted the invite and was sitting around the pool when I recognized one of the guests as Roy Cohn, Senator McCarthy's right hand man (Mr. Blacklist himself). We struck up a conversation; he knew who I was and was aware of what had happened to me. After a pleasant afternoon's talk about matters non-political, he stood up to leave, shook my hand and said, "You're a really nice guy. Too bad we have to kill you."

Shortly after that, true to his word, Ed Sullivan called. Roy Cohn notwithstanding, the blacklist was beginning to wane. TV producers had become sick of the extortion racket, which is what it really was, and Sullivan was able to book me on his show once more. I loved Ed. America did too. He was a good guy. He read from cue cards, but never learned to . master the technique When the Singing Nun was on his show, performing her hit record, Ed read, "Because Sister Dominique is a member of the order of the Carmelite Nuns, she is unable to accept our usual recompense. So, in lieu of the traditional stipend, we are presenting her convent with a Jew." There was a terrible pause, and Ed looked back down at his cue card. "I'm sorry," he said. "A Jeep."

I fell for a Broadway dancer and married her. Eighteen months later, we had a baby. When the little girl was a year old, the dancer announced that she had met her soul mate, a Frenchman, and ran off to Africa with him, leaving the baby behind. I guess it was pretty romantic, but at the time it didn't seem that way to me. I had my little girl though, and loved her. The dancer had hired a live-in mother's helper, a beautiful seventeen year old Irish girl named Bridey. I kept her on the payroll and the three of us cohabited in an odd, platonic ménage. I had a larger apartment overlooking the East River by then.

I became a regular on the game show To Tell the Truth and stayed on that program for seven years, sitting between Kitty Carlisle and Peggy Cass. I came to love the raspy-voiced Peggy (I called her the ward-heeler's daughter) and the elegant Kitty, who sometimes wore a feather boa. Kitty was married to Moss Hart, the Broadway director of My Fair Lady and Camelot. She lived high off the hog in a duplex apartment on Park Avenue, but always remained a simple girl at heart. She told me that on the occasion of her and Moss' twenty-fifth anniversary, they had dined alone at home, sitting at a dining room table which could seat sixteen. As the butler tip-toed out of the room, Moss reached over, took his wife's hand, and said, "Well, Kitty. You've stuck with me through *thick*."

XV

I began to appear on the Tonight Show, and over time I became the regular substitute host, filling in for Jack Paar. Paar was an odd, moody guy who wore his feelings on his sleeve. What you saw was what you got. If he was in a snit, he did nothing to conceal it. Yet people would ask, "What's Jack Paar really like?" Sub-hosts on Tonight got to pick their own guests (at least, I did). There had never been a Black stand-up comic on the show (on any network show, I think). I urged the management to book Nipsey Russell. They didn't resist; no-one had pushed for it before. Nipsey did great.

One night I wandered into a boite in the Village and saw a young woman with the voice of an angel and a honk the size of a cucumber. Barbra was nineteen, had had a fight with her mother, and was without a place to sleep. I had a manager (I was his only client). I made a call and prevailed upon him to let Barbra crash on the couch in his office. I was scheduled to host the Tonight Show that week, and I asked the producers to book her as a guest performer.

"Some unknown kid?" they complained. But I kept pushing and they finally agreed. In her first-ever appearance on TV, she sang "When a Bee Lies Sleeping in the Palm of your Hand" and brought the studio audience to its feet.

I was a guest on the night Paar famously walked off the Tonight Show, saying that he would never come back. He had had a beef with NBC over the censoring of one of his jokes. Twenty minutes into the program, he made his announcement to a stunned studio audience, and left. Nobody on the production staff knew about his plans; the producer and director were taken totally by surprise. The other guests and I on the show did the best we could to carry on without him. Tape had been invented and the program was recorded at five in the afternoon for an eleven thirty showing. All the seven o'clock network news programs broke the story that Paar would quit during the show, and that viewers could see for themselves when it aired that night. They watched in record numbers.

I stuck up for Paar on the air that night, having been on the receiving end of censorship myself. (Paar flew to Hong Kong, had a vacation, and was back on the air a week later.) The network was not pleased with my remarks, and I was taken out of the running to replace him when eventually he did retire. Johnny Carson, who had been emceeing an afternoon quiz show called Who Do You Trust, was hired for the job, and I continued to sub-host, doing the job over a hundred times.

In '64 I starred with Paul Ford and Maureen O'Sullivan in a comedy called *Never Too Late*. It turned out to be the biggest success I had on Broadway, running almost three years. In the plot Ford, a middle-aged business man, is married to the beautiful and charming O'Sullivan. I played their ne'r-do-well son-in-law (who lives with them, and whom Ford cannot stand). Maureen comes home one day with the ecstatic news that, twenty years after the birth of their daughter, she is pregnant again. She is in bliss, Ford is in shock, thinking only of the ridicule he is sure they'll heap on him down at the lumber yard he runs.

Lost in her own, euphoric reverie, the wife murmurs, "What's that poem, Harry?"

"I shot an arrow into the air," answers her husband. The laugh went on for a full minute.

A year into the run, Maureen O'Sullivan's husband, the film director John Farrow, died. Their daughter, the beautiful 18 year old Mia, had been in boarding school in Switzerland. With the family in upheaval, she returned home to America to live with her mom, and started hanging out backstage at the theater. I had taken over a little suite of dressing rooms on the third floor. The star dressing rooms downstairs were occupied by Paul and Maureen. The younger members of the cast and their understudies took to hanging out in my digs. Maureen's daughter joined them.

Mia Farrow became my daughter's matinee baby sitter. Back before it was the trendy thing to do, I was raising my little girl as a single parent. How I adored her. Pretty Irish Bridey would drop her off at the theater on Wednesday and Saturday matinee days, and take the afternoon off. Mia would look after her when

I was acting on stage. After the performance I would take my sweet girl across the street to the Absinthe House restaurant, order a steak for myself, and a kiddy meal for her. Then we'd cab uptown to our apartment, I'd drop her off with Bridey, and return to the theater for my evening performance.

One post-matinee evening in the Absinthe House, my daughter, terrible-two-and-a-half years old, got up from her seat next to me and began meandering around the restaurant, talking to other diners. At first, they found the precocious little girl adorable. *At first.* I had ordered our dinners and was waiting for the waiter to bring them. I called to my daughter to stop pestering people and come sit down. She paid no attention. I called to her a couple of more times. She stubbornly refused to stop. The customers were being polite, but I could see they were getting annoyed (other people's children…). I summoned the waiter.

"I'd like my check, please."

"But Mr. Bean, you haven't eaten yet.

"That's OK, Please bring me the bill; we're leaving." I paid for our unconsumed dinners and we cabbed home unfed, my little girl in tears.

"I told you, honey, that you had to stop bothering people. You have to do what I tell you. If you want to go to restaurants with me, those are the rules. Bridey will get you something to eat at home." It was the best steak I never ate. I had no problems in public with her again; when I told her to behave, she knew I meant it.

Being a single parent caused me to ruminate about how to raise a child. I didn't like the authoritarian approach (be good or you'll get spanked). But I hated permissiveness. It seemed to produce spoiled brats. There had to be, I thought, a better way. I was already trying to home school my little girl. When she was three, I taught her to read by taping 3X5 cards all over our apartment. The word COUCH was on the couch, TABLE on the table. I had read about the technique in a magazine.

She had a little friend she liked to play with in the next apartment to ours. One day, she came home in tears.

"Emily says I'm going to die," she sobbed.

"What?!"

"Emily says I'm going to die. She says everybody is going to die."

"Well, I'm not."

"But Emily says…"

"Who are you going to believe, me or Emily? I tell you I'm not going to die."

"Can you just say that?"

"Sure"

"You can just *say* that?"

"Yes. I'm saying it. Are you?"

"Well sure, if you can just say that."

"Okay, then. It's a deal. We're not going to die and to heck with Emily." My daughter was vastly relieved and the subject was dropped.

Never Too Late put on an Actor's Fund performance. All Broadway shows did them once a year on (otherwise dark) Sunday nights to raise money for "our own charity", the Old Actors' Retirement Home. It was a chance for working performers to see the shows that were playing at the same time as theirs were. When the curtain came down, an actress I knew slightly, Margot Moser, showed up at my dressing room She was the current Eliza Doolittle in My Fair Lady, having replaced whoever had taken over for Julie Andrews. She offered the obligatory praise of my acting prowess, then handed me a book.

"Take a look at this," she said. Her eyes were gleaming with excitement.

"What is it?"

"It's called Summerhill. That's the name of a school in England, which is unique and special. We want to start one like it here in the states."

"What is it, an acting school?"

"No, no. It's a school for children. It's different from any other school in the world." Margot knew I was raising my little girl on my own. "There's nothing like it, " she said, "Kids learn to take responsibility for their own lives."

"Why are you so interested in that?"

"Oh, I don't know. Maybe I just want to save the world." She threw back her head and laughed, then indicated the book in my hand. "Promise me you'll read it, Orson. Then call me." She handed me a slip of paper with her phone number on it.

"I'll take a look,"

"Promise? This is important."

"Okay, okay, Margot".

She gave me a peck on the cheek and left. I grabbed a cab and went straight home. Bridey normally had Sunday nights off, but because of the benefit performance, she'd had to stay in and baby-sit. She left the apartment as soon as I showed up at eleven, heading for a club on east 96th Street where Irish nannies liked to congregate on their nights off. I peeked in at my daughter; she was fast asleep. I touched her cheek and got a lump in my throat. Her whole life lay ahead of her, and it was in my power to help shape it. I popped open a can of beer, carried it to the easy chair by my window that looked out on the East River, and opened the book Margot had given me.

It was written by an old Scotsman named A. S. Neill and told the story of a boarding school he'd been running in England for sixty years. The school, like the book, was called Summerhill. Neill advocated maximum freedom combined with maximum personal responsibility. His slogan was "freedom, not license". He argued that children, even very young ones, can learn to take responsibility for their own lives.

As I read on, (quaffing a second can of Bud), I began to understand why Margot Moser had seemed so excited. The approach Neill advocated really was unique. Kids can be scared into behaving by "spare the rod...", he wrote, or they can get away with *not* behaving, when raised by permissive parents. He postulated that a rational discipline (not one based on patriarchal authoritarianism) *appeals* to children, who have a natural need for boundaries. As I read on, I started to get as excited as Margot had seemed to be.

I phoned the next day to tell her my reaction. She explained that there was a group of people who had come together in hopes of starting a school in New York City. She had joined the organization, which met from time to time... and as it happened, there was a get-together coming up that week. I took down the info and told her I'd be there.

At the meeting, I learned that the publisher of Summerhill had included a postcard in each copy of the book, asking readers if they wished to participate in organizing a school in America. The folks at the meeting had sent their cards in, and there was a list of other people who had done so. There was excitement in the air; a sense that something really important might be about to take place.

I signed up to join the group and began attending their meetings. This went on for the best part of a year. The discussions were endless. Money was raised to buy a property, plans were talked about, but nobody really seemed to take action and nothing ever got done. It gradually dawned on me that, while the *idea* of opening a Summerhill-type school appealed tremendously to the devotees in the group, actually doing something about it seemed to be less attractive.

A radical notion began to take shape in my mind. My little girl would soon be old enough to start school and I wanted nothing more than to be able to send her to one like A. S. Neill's. My life was good; I was one of the fortunate ones, and felt obliged to give something back to the world. I had thirty five thousand bucks saved up from what I'd earned on Broadway and television. I decided that, even though I knew absolutely nothing about how to run a school, I would see if I could open one. I had visions of saving the world by populating it with young people who would grow up knowing how to take responsibility for themselves.

It had always been my nature to take risks, to put the cart before the horse and plunge into unknown territory. An acquaintance put me in touch with a realtor, a woman with the unlikely name of Sugar Cane. Sugar was a go-getter and promptly came across an old union hall which had just come on the market. It was located on the fringes of Greenwich Village on Fifteenth Street in Manhattan, It had been the headquarters of a small, left-wing teachers union, which had, in its day, fought militantly for teachers rights and believed that it had influenced the larger union to be stronger. But by now its members were old and tired and ready to turn in.

The asking price for the four story fire-proof structure was $87,500 and thirty five grand would do just fine as a down payment. The building had a large meeting hall on the ground floor which I thought, when Sugar took me on the tour, would do just fine as a combination gym and auditorium There were classrooms on the upper floors, rest rooms in the basement and a roof which could be fenced in to function as a playground. Sugar negotiated a deal, papers were signed and in no time the building was mine. I applied for and was given a provisional charter by the state of New York, and set about getting in touch with teachers. The publishers of the book Summerhill kindly shared the list of the people who had sent in cards expressing interest in starting a school.

I sent out a mailing announcing that a Sumerhillian school would be opening in September, and on a hot July evening, a hundred people assembled in the unions meeting hall. That night, miraculously, thirty nine sets of parents and four qualified teachers signed on to the experiment. We opened for business on September 6th, 1965, with 40 students enrolled in kindergarten and grades one, two and three. My dear daughter was one of the charter members (it was for her that I had really started the school).

The ratio of kids to teachers was ten to one. The plan was to add a grade each year until the school reached K through 6 and had a hundred kids and ten teachers. I functioned (while keeping on with my show business career) as general administrator, leaving the actual imparting of education to the teachers, each of whom had Masters Degrees. They were excited about doing something new and experimental, and all of them were willing to take less money than they could have made working for the city. The school had opened its doors within six months of my decision to purchase a building.

The Summerhill approach functioned, in practical terms, in the following way: reading class was offered at ten, math class at eleven, i.e.. Attendance at class was not mandatory. If a kid chose not to attend, he could hang out in the gym or go up on the roof to the playground. Or he could wander the halls with a comic book in his hand. What he could not do was sit in the classroom while studies were being taught and cause disruption. So, the teachers could concentrate on teaching, rather than having to police behavior.

The other rule was that, having elected not to go to class, a kid couldn't change his mind after a week or so, and expect automatically to be let in. This would cause extra work for the teacher, and take time away from the kids who had come from the beginning. A big majority of students chose to attend class. A few did not. These, when classes were in session, sat on the floor of the gym and looked at comic books, or drew on scrap paper... or shot hoops with a basket ball on the roof. After a while, most of the non-attenders became bored and told their teacher that they had decided to try going to class.

"No way," the teacher would answer. "I haven't got time to catch you up"

"But that's not fair. I've got nothing to do."

"I'll see if I can get one of the other kids to help you. If it turns out you can cut the mustard and not hold things up, maybe we'll let you into the class." It became quite common to see two children sitting on the floor of the cloakroom with books in their laps, the one instructing the other, both benefiting. Getting an education, they were finding out, was a privilege to be earned, not a right they were entitled to.

In the sixteen year history of the school, we estimated that out of the hundreds of kids who attended, only four wound up never attending any class at all. And each of these, we found, had learned, in some way the teachers never understood, to read, write and count just as well as the others... apparently by osmosis, just by being around an atmosphere where learning was taking place. The teachers never could figure out how it had worked (it helped them avoid having excessive professional pride).

Joey Gallo's wife (beautiful and brainy, of course) showed up with the mobster's young son one day, looking to enroll him. We were quite taken with the boy and accepted him at once. But Mrs. Gallo called back the next day, saying that unfortunately she had to decline. Joey had said, "How do I know the kid's gonna get into Harvard if they don't make him learn nothing'".

During the third year of the running of The Fifteenth Street School, when I was hosting the Tonight Show, I talked NBC into bringing A. S. Neill over from England to be a guest. I had visited and gotten to know him (and see Summerhill) shortly before having started the project. The network flew the old man across the Atlantic first class, and he was the best guest the program ever had: "Suffer little children to come unto me...and get a good lickin'."

Never Too Late continued to run on Broadway. My grandfather, now a vital 89, came to New York to visit me. After 60 years of marriage, my grandmother had passed away and grandpa was on the loose again. I introduced him to the 18-year old Mia Farrow and they hit it off. Grandpa asked her out and they went dancing at Roseland. He stayed two weeks and I saw very little of him; he and Mia had bonded. Just before he left for Vermont, he told me that he was really taken with her. "If I was only seventy again…" I didn't have the heart to tell him that Justice Brandeis had already used the line.

Neil Simon asked me to star in *The Odd Couple* opposite my old stage-mate, Walter Matthou. I said no; really dumb career move. I had been asked to replace Anthony Newly in *The Roar of the Greasepaint*, which was continuing its run at the Shubert Theater; I had been studying singing and wanted to keep doing musicals. There was a giant in the show. Newly was eccentric and went for odd casting choices. The giant attached himself to me. It turned out he was an intellectual, like the one at The Palace, and tried to talk philosophy. I figured there must be something about me that makes smart giants want to befriend me.

The giant told me he had had traveled with the Ringling Brothers, Barnum and Bailey Circus. In the course of Greasepaint's run, they called and wanted him to come back. He said yes and gave notice. Who would want to travel with a circus and be in a sideshow, when he could appear in a Broadway musical? Apparently the giant did.

"They're going to have to close the show", I thought. "How can they find another giant?" The producer, David Merrick, put out a casting call and asked me to read with the new giant, as I had a scene with the character in the production. I said sure, but didn't think I'd really have to do it, as they weren't going to find anyone.

On a Thursday afternoon at four, Shubert Alley was filled with giants. There must have been fifteen or twenty of them. I couldn't believe my eyes. In the show, the giant picks my character up and walks down a steep rake toward the front of the stage. This was a little dangerous, so the stage manager said I could read the lines in the auditions, but then he, the stage manager, would be the one the giant would carry. Giants are not known for their physical strength, so they had to be sure the giant they cast was up to the task.

I read with some of the giants and the director selected a few they thought were thespians. Then the stage manager and one of the giants climbed to the top of the raked stage. He hopped up into the big guy's arms and they started their descent...a little too fast. "Slow down," said the stage manager. The giant did not slow down. His eyes were glazed over. I thought of a toy I'd had as a kid, a wooden cow with movable legs which you could put on a large book, an Atlas or something, propped up to be on a slant, and the cow would walk down the book.

"Slower," the stage manager said again, starting to panic. The giant kept going. He seemed to be in a daze. "Stop!" yelled the poor stage manager. As I watched, the two of them went off the front of the stage and straight down onto the orchestra pit.

Neither one was hurt, thank God, but auditions were called off for the rest of the day.

I finished my ten years of analysis, and felt ten years older and thousands of dollars poorer. Undaunted, I began what turned out to be two years of Reichian therapy. Reich had been one of Freud's young Turks in Vienna. He split with the master, when he came to believe in something called Orgone energy, which he believed to be the life force. Reich was the grand-daddy of all the touchy-feely therapies which came along in the sixties. Rolfing (I was actually rolfed by Ida Rolf herself; it hurt like hell.), Bio-energetics, and Primal Scream were all started by patients of Reich's and were variations of his therapy. Subsequent to the Orgone stuff, I did EST, Werner Ehrhart's conglomerate of everything out there. I did Re-birthing. I walked on fire. If I didn't do a self-improvement of some kind, it was because I hadn't heard of it. I was determined to become happy.

Love came into my life. I had decided that I needed a wife and my little girl needed a mother. At a bar called Sparks Pub, not far from my apartment, I spied a beautiful young woman. She was sitting at a table with a girl friend, looking for all the world as if she owned the joint. I moved in like a Kansas City burglar, brazenly sat down next to her like it was the most natural thing in the world, and began to interview her as if she were applying for a job and I was the boss. She was a dress-maker, it seemed, and told me she was a good one. I liked that. I asked her out. The second time we dated, I introduced her to my five year old. They hit it off. I courted slowly, wary after what had happened before.

———•·•———

In time, I decided I wanted to make the woman mine. But I had to get my daughter's permission first; she'd had me all to herself for a long time. When I broached the subject, she had a question.

"Who do you love best, me or her?"

"I love you best as a daughter and I love her best as a girlfriend."

"But who do you love *best*?" She wasn't going to settle. I talked it over with my Reichian shrink, a very wise man.

"Tell your daughter you love her best," he said,

"But isn't that psychologically iffy?"

"That's what most therapists would tell you. But think about it. What's easier to give up, something you've *had*... or something you've always longed for and never had? Give her what she needs. She'll let go of it when she grows up and meets her own guy."

The next time I brought up the subject of marriage with my little girl, she asked me the usual question. I looked around conspiratorially.

"I love you best," I said. "But let's not tell her. We don't want to hurt her feelings." Her five year old face lit up.

"Alright, you can marry her," she said. "Do I get to be flower girl?"

———•·•———

She did get to be flower girl. The beautiful dress-maker said yes. The year was 1965. Grandpa came down from Vermont for the wedding. My Uncle Gene's kids came; they were the only other relatives I had, except for my father. I agonized over inviting him and decided not to. His and my grandfather's relationship had been strained at best, and I wanted the old man to relax and enjoy himself. The bride's people came, and a lot of friends. I had moved to a carriage house on McDougal Alley in Greenwich Village, and that's where we got married. The ceremony was performed by Al Carmines, the minister of Judson Memorial Church, a Greenwich Village institution more concerned with Nicaragua than with Jesus. The wedding guests dined on Chinese food.

A year later our first son was born. We brought him home from the hospital. My then six year old daughter cast a gimlet eye on the new arrival, then pulled me aside.

"You remember that deal we made?" she said. I had no idea what she was talking about.

"What deal?"

"That deal that we weren't going to die."

"Oh, that deal. Yeah, I remember it."

"We don't have to let him in on that."

———•———

The dressmaker and I bought a house on the fringes of Greenwich Village in Manhattan. (Actually, it was on the same block as the school, and my bride took over the day-to-day running of the administrative office, our baby lying in a basket beside her desk.) The house was a hundred years old. The dressmaker drew up plans, and we re-did it from top to bottom. She gave birth again, to a little girl this time. Our ménage included a live-in au pair (English), a full time maid and a guy named Warren, who came twice a week to do the heavy cleaning. Warren put on a white jacket and acted as butler when we gave dinner parties.

Like the one we gave for William F. Buckley and his wife Patricia. Knowing that Buckley would be bored by the company of conservatives who agreed with him, I invited Mike Wallace and Fried Friendly, the honcho of CBS news, to dine with the Buckleys. I could ask people like that to dinner because I had become famous and, as S. J. Perelman has written, "There are no strangers in the aristocracy of success."

For the next five years I acted in theater and on television. I ran the school. I taped To Tell the Truth five times a week, appeared on talk shows, and became the voice for Manufacturers Trust TV commercials. I produced an Obie winning off-Broadway play, Home Movies. I recorded an album of original songs called You're a Good Man, Charlie Brown, singing the title role. Charles Schulz himself supervised the recording. (The album spawned the stage show.) I recorded a comedy album entitled I Ate the Baloney. I wrote a book about my experience in Reichian therapy: Me and the Orgone, submitted it to St. Martins Press and they accepted it for publication.

I had little time to sleep and learned to do without much of it; I was running on fumes. When I tried to answer fan mail on Sundays, my only time off, the beautiful dressmaker put her foot down. You have to rest, she said, and made me relax or take her out to dinner. My career was exploding. The New York Times wrote about the school I had started. Look Magazine published a picture story that showed our students teaching one another. People stopped me in the street and asked for my autograph. I smiled at them and signed the pieces of paper they offered me. The year was 1970; I was forty two. It was all too much. I was coming apart at the seams.

———•———

The times were overtly political. The Viet Nam war was raging. The Weathermen had built a bomb factory in the basement of a fancy townhouse that belonged to the parents of one of them on west 11th Street, a few blocks from where my family was living. One of the bombs went off and blew up the place, killing three of the apprentice terrorists in the process. Our house, four blocks away, shook severely when we heard the explosion. I walked over and took a look at the smoldering ruins. My old pal, Dusty Hoffman, who had become a movie star by then, lived next door. A big hole was ripped out of his place.

Revolution was in the air. The wail of sirens was heard incessantly in Manhattan. Radicals were turning in false alarms just to "screw up the system." The fire department didn't dare ignore the alarms, so the streets were filled with fire trucks. I was exhausted but didn't know it. Voices began to reverberate in my head: "Get out, get out, get out." What did the evacuation message mean? My life was a superfluity of good things.

I began, oddly enough, to dream of escaping to Australia. Here in America, the generals were meeting in secret; this was my fantasy. They would not tolerate the anarchy which was starting to erupt. The country would go fascist. (Can you say Mid-life Crisis?)

———•◦•———

Producers from Down Under came to New York to cast the leads for a production of the musical, *Promises, Promises*. A plan began to formulate in what could laughingly be referred to as my mind: I would run away from home and take the family with me. I told my idea to the beautiful dressmaker. She loved our life. She loved New York. She loved the home she'd designed for us, she loved running the school office. She was a "good wife" and capitulated to her husbands wishes.

I auditioned for *Promises, Promises* by learning a song from the show's score and singing it on the Merv Griffin Show. I told my agent to ask the Aussie producers to watch it. They did, and offered me the job. I told a very unhappy Mark Goodson I was leaving To Tell the Truth.

———•◦•———

The always reliable Sugar Cane put our place on the market. Potential buyers came, inspected our home and declined. We began to wonder if we were going to be able to sell it (best house on a so-so block). When we had first bought the place and re-designed it, I had told the contractor that I wanted him to build me a secret passage: a boyhood dream from all those Universal Frankenstein movies. The entrance to the passage was behind a wall mirror. The passageway snaked between walls and exited through a sliding panel in another room of the house.

One day, Sugar showed up with a rich lady who had a kid in tow: a spoiled and surly eight year old boy. No, he didn't wanna look around the house, he wasn't interested; he'd sit and watch TV while the realtor took his mother on the guided tour. I approached the boy.

"Hey, kid. You wanna see something weird?"

"What?"

"C'mere with me." We walked into the other room. "Press this button on the wall." The mirror slid to one side. The kids eyes popped. He crept into the passageway. The mirror closed behind him. I moved down the hall to the room into which the passageway exited.

From inside the wall: "How do you get outa here?"

"Push the panel" The kid came out wide-eyed, then ran looking for his mother. "Mom, mom, look at this!" We sold the house that day for our asking price.

The time came for the family to leave and begin our new lives down under. I had become convinced that the generals would march on Washington, D.C. (and take control of the country) on July 4th, a symbolic date, so I booked the family on a flight to Australia on July 3rd. At the last minute, we were invited to a swell 4th of July party, so I changed the reservations to the fifth. That's how crazy I was.

I turned the running of the school over to the teachers, one of whom, Patty Green, assumed the role of managing director. By the time it finally closed its doors, so many other schools around the country had been influenced by it, that it no longer needed to exist.

The Bean family flew down under, stopping on the way for a week's rest on the island of Fiji. The men wear skirts there. The traffic cop we saw in the capitol city of Suva sported a military jacket with epaulettes, a Sam Brown belt and pistol, but with a skirt underneath. We stayed at a fancy hotel called the Fijian. The locals were the friendliest people I had ever met in my life. After years in New York City, I was immediately suspicious; what did they want? I received an education that week: all they wanted was to be friendly.

I had a Polaroid camera, one of the earliest models, a big clunker. The family strolled off the hotel grounds one day, and into a tribal village. The chief offered us drinks of Kava, a local delicacy. He invited us into his fancy straw hut. I took his picture with the Polaroid. He was used to having his photo shot by tourists. What he was not used to was holding a blank square of something in his hand and, very gradually watching his image appear in it. He became wild with excitement. We had to take Polaroid shots of every member of the tribe.

At lunch in the hotel dining room one day, we looked out the window and saw a tour bus pull up. A banner on the side proclaimed that it had been chartered by The Australian Maimed and Limbless Society. Our hearts sank. The door of the bus opened, and out poured a cavalcade of the afflicted: amputees and the Cerebral Palsied. They had come, as we had, to enjoy a week's vacation. They made their way into the dining room, stashing crutches, walkers and wheel chairs by the front door, enquiring as to whether it was too late to eat lunch. The place suddenly looked like Lourdes.

All the guests in the dining room, as we watched this spectacle, were made one by wildly conflicting thoughts. The decent, Christian-like parts of us thought, "How nice that these unfortunates can enjoy some time on this beautiful island." The nasty, evil, human parts of us thought: "Why this hotel? Why the week that *we're* here?" We all politely pretended not to notice the new arrivals.

That afternoon, as my family and I sat on a towel on the beautiful white sand by the ocean, one of the new arrivals, a severely palsied young man appeared, making his way along the beach as best he could. My son, now six, pointed at him.

"Look at the way he's walking," he said.

"Shh," I told him. "Don't point at him. Don't talk about it."

"But why is he walking that way?"

"I don't know. Stop pointing at him. It's rude." Before we could stop him, he had jumped up and run to the young man. We watched in horror.

"Why do you walk so funny?" asked my son.

"Only way I can walk, mate. Wanna take a walk with me?" Of course he did, and off they went together, along the sand. My wife and I looked at each other in shame. We had acted as if nothing was wrong with these people, effectively cutting them off from any connection to us. My "rude" little boy had made a friend. (They did, in fact, become pals for the remaining days we were there.)

Promises, Promises rehearsed and then opened in Melbourne, Australia, after which it moved to Sydney. During the run, we (I) decided to settle in and buy a house overlooking the harbor. What was I looking to be in Australia: a big frog in a small puddle? I wasn't sure. Why had I done what I had done? America had not gone fascist; I could read the papers. What was going on with me?

Promises, Promises finished a successful, six month run and, back in the states, my book, Me and the Orgone, was set to appear in stores. St. Martin's Press flew me to New York for ten days to help promote it. The book proved to be quite a success, going into multiple printings (more than forty years later, it is still in print). While I was autographing copies in a Manhattan outlet, I picked up a book from the New Non-Fiction table: The Greening of America (anybody remember that one?).

I read it on the plane on the way back down under and it quite simply blew my mind. I realized that what had induced me to give up my career and the house and everything it represented, was not what I had imagined; I had told myself America was coming apart and that I needed to get away. But what I had needed to get away from, I now knew, was something inside of me. For all of my adult life, I had pursued the bitch goddess success... with a vengeance. And really, I asked myself, what had it all come to? (Aside from the school. That, I was proud of.)

A new consciousness took me over: I would radically simplify my life. Too much was not enough, and henceforth I decided I would live in the much heralded "now". I announced to the poor, long-suffering Mrs. Bean that we were about to begin a new chapter of the soap opera we called our life. We had spent a year and a half in Australia. She had designed and supervised the building of yet another beautiful home, which she would now have to abandon. We'd had another baby, a little boy (conceived in Melbourne where the pubs closed early back then, and there wasn't much else to do after dark). It was time to go home.

We put the Sydney house on the market and flew back to the states. We had left with three children; we came back with four. We landed in New York City and stayed with friends. I saw an old Volkswagen bus parked on a street in Greenwich Village. It had a sign in the window saying that the owner would sell it for five hundred dollars. I bought it.

We chugged across the country, stopping to look at the Grand Canyon. The money from the sale of the Australia house came through and we used it to buy a place in L. A. No more Broadway for me. No more busting my hump to make a living. I figured Johnny Carson would book me on his show at least once a month, I could pick up a few game shows and that would bring in enough to live on. House brand Frosted Flakes tasted just fine.

Thunder clouds. At long last, the beautiful dressmaker got sick of being dragged all over the globe by the lunatic she had married, and decided she'd had enough. I had burned our candle at both ends and charred our life irreparably. The marriage had lasted sixteen years. What happened, in nutshell (no pun intended), was that despite a decade of analysis, two years of Orgone therapy, Est and rebirthing, I never was able to overcome my childhood trauma. I did not believe, deep down, that I was loveable. So, despite all evidence to the contrary, I could not accept that she loved me, and, in one way after another, I had alienated her.

When life came crashing down around me, and I realized what my craziness had led to, I was devastated. It took me ten years to get over the loss of her. I became bi-coastal, moving back to New York and commuting to L.A. to spend time with my beloved children. It was 1980.

I was entering into a very dark decade of my life.

XVI

As a boy, I used to think about Dallas Lund. If my
mother had married the can opener magnate, that's the
name her son would have been given. I know she would
have named him Dallas because it was her father's name
and she adored him. That's why she named me Dallas.

What would Dallas Lund's life have been like? Surely,
he would have been a happy little boy; my mother was
carefree when she was in Vermont with her family. It
was only after she met and dedicated her life to my
father, that she started down the road that led to the
gas oven at twelve Wright Street.

Dallas Lund's mother would have held him on her
lap while she read to him. When his father came home
from work at night, she'd have dinner ready; perhaps
it would already be on the table. Maybe dad would
have a cocktail while he told his family about the new
inventions he had come up with that day. Mom would
clap her hands in delight and tell him they sounded
wonderful and that he was truly making the world

a better place. Ed Lund would laugh and pick little Dallas up, toss him in the air and catch him. Dallas would laugh, too.

Little Dallas Lund would have whatever he wanted; his father was rich, after all. The family would live in a fine big house in Burlington at first, but when dad's business expanded, they'd move to Atlanta, where the big new factory was. Dallas would not have to wash windows, mow lawns or sell Gebott's Crème Friedcakes to save up money to buy a used bicycle. His parents would give him a new one when he asked for it, with ribbons on the ends of the handlebars. They'd love him so much that they'd give him everything he asked for. When he grew up and began dating girls, if a girl didn't give him what he wanted, he would say to himself, "Doesn't she know who I am?" and move on to another girl.

When the war came, Dallas Lund wouldn't wait to be drafted, he'd already be in college, and would join the Reserve Officers Training Corp. When he graduated, he'd be given lieutenant's bars. Everyone would say how handsome he looked in his uniform. He'd be sent overseas and on his first day in combat; he'd be hit by a mortar shell and get killed.

My earliest memory of a religious education of any kind, is of being taken by my grandparents to the little church they attended in Hartland, Vermont. I don't recall their mentioning God around the house, but they went to church on Sundays, where they met with friends and exchanged pleasantries. Dr. Forkell was the preacher. He had not been endowed by his Creator with a particular gift for communication. He spoke, on the Sunday I recall, of the requirement that we feel love in our hearts for all our fellow creatures. Leaning forward for emphasis, he added, "and that includes the summer people." As I sat day-dreaming in the pew next to my mother, I fantasized that I was a little Pilgrim boy, that the preacher was Cotton Mather, and that a man with a long pole with a knob on the end of it would bop me on the noggin if I drifted off.

My grandmother tried to attend to my moral education, using children's picture books like *The Grasshopper and the Ant*. In the illustrations, the little red ant wore overalls and toiled all day long. The grasshopper sported a spiffy green suit. and looked like a city slicker. He smiled engagingly as he lazed about, watching the ant work. But when the winter came, the ant sat in his little house in an easy chair in front of a cheery blaze in his fireplace. He had a warm cup of something in his hand. Outside, the grasshopper, whose green suit was now threadbare and whose shoes were coming apart, banged on the ant's door, begging to be let in from the cold. In the picture, he was shivering, clutching his ragged coat to his breast.

"Please let me in," he cries. "I'll freeze!"

"No," says the ant. ""You played all summer while I worked, Now you must pay the price."

"Death," I asked my grandmother? She nodded solemnly. I, of course, identified completely with the grasshopper. I wanted to play all summer. The little red ant (a Communist, I wondered, like my father's gabby friends down in Cambridge?) seemed dour and unfunny to me. I wanted to be funny. My grandmother closed the picture book and looked at me as if to ensure that the moral had soaked in. But every summer in Hartland, there were just as many grasshoppers hopping around as there had been the year before. Something was wrong here.

The Three Little Pigs was another of my un-favorites. The third pig, with the house of brick, was just as unattractive to me as the ant had been. Work hard and you get to look after your slothful brothers; that was the moral I took away from the tale. At the Peabody School, when I was ten or eleven, we were given stories to read with titles like *The Spartan Boy*. In that one, a boy steals a fox cub, hides it under his jacket (toga?) and takes it to school with him. It begins to claw him, but rather than ruin his reputation by revealing the theft, he does not cry out. Ultimately, the fox cub claws the boy to death. The moral? I couldn't figure it out. Death before dishonor? It made me feel vaguely guilty, that's all I know. Okay to steal a fox; not good to cop to it?

In one of the paperbacks I read in Philadelphia, a book on astronomy, I learned that if stars were reduced to the size of pin-points, only three of them would fit inside the Grand Central Station. That's how enormous the distances are between them. All throughout my childhood, I looked up at the heavens at night and wondered, wondered, wondered. Today, I know (we all know) about the Big Bang, about how everything came into existence at that moment. Including time. What happened to time travel, which I used to read about in Astounding Science Fiction in my hotel room? If time is always moving forward from the moment of that big explosion (which science largely agrees is the case), there can be no going backwards or forwards, because it's always now. It's now *now*. And now it's now. Two seconds from now, it will still be now. I can ask myself, "What will happen tomorrow morning? What will I do then?" But the time never comes when I hop out of bed and cry, "At last, it's then!" It will still be now. The same now it is now.

This is the kind of stuff I think about, and always have done. Everything began at the moment of the Big Bang. Before that, there was nothing. No time, no space, no nothing. So if that's true, and most of the experts agree that it is, who lit the fuse and set the whole thing off, like a Macy's fireworks display? If everything in the natural universe began at a precise moment, whatever existed before that moment has to be *super*natural. If within the first few seconds after the Big Bang, all the elements appeared (helium, hydrogen, etc.) which were needed to create everything that subsequently followed: space, matter, black holes, stars, spiral nebulae, planets, climate change, one-celled organisms, lung fish, dinosaurs, saber toothed tigers and finally, for good or ill, people...that sounds like Cosmic City Planning to me.

I remember Mr. Bartlett, the biology teacher at Cambridge High and Latin. He discusses the transformation of caterpillar into butterfly. "What's the process that goes on inside a cocoon?" he asks. "Has anyone ever seen a picture of the insect at the halfway point between caterpillar and butterfly? " No one has. The next week, Mr. Bartlett finds a cocoon in the woods and brings it to the classroom. We crowd around, as he takes a single edged blade and neatly slices it in two. The cocoon looks empty.

"There's nothing in there," says one of the kids.

"Oh, it's in there," says Mr. Bartlett. "It just doesn't have a shape right now. The living, breathing material is spun right into the sides of the cocoon. Caterpillar is gone; butterfly is yet to come." We stare in wonder.

"Real transformation," says Mr. Bartlett, "means giving up one form before you can have another. It requires the willingness to be nothing for a while."

XVII

New York City 1980

Bleak, black despair. Divorce final, career in shambles, kids a coast away. Staring out the window of my small west side Manhattan apartment for hours on end. I do an occasional job, then retreat to the pad and sit. Just sit. I've had one wall of the living room lined with mirrors to make it look less narrow than it is. There's a walk-in (barely) kitchen, a bathroom so miniscule I have to go outside to change my mind, and a tiny bedroom. I'm nearly catatonic. Can't concentrate enough even to watch TV. Can't sit through a movie. Can't, won't, don't go to a bar. Don't want to talk to anyone. I live on the thirty-fourth floor of a brand new building. I am, in fact, the only tenant in the whole place. It isn't completed yet (the lower floors aren't finished), but the management is taking orders and telling people they can move in after a month or two. I tell them I didn't care, let me move in now. They say alright and take my money. Looking south over nothing but tenements, I can see the Empire State Building and beyond that, on a clear day, the Twin Towers.

It's summer. On weekends, the fancy people are away, gone to the Hamptons. I spend most afternoons in Central Park, a block east from me, an easy walk. The park is pretty scruffy in 1980. They haven't fixed it up yet, or started keeping the cars out. I sit on a bench and watch the tourists, or I walk through the sheep meadow and down to the lake. I bring peanuts and feed the squirrels. I grab a hotdog from a Sabrett cart and wash it down with a bottle of Yoohoo. I pick up something to cook for dinner from Gristede's and retreat back to my lair. I write to the kids every other day.

One evening around 7:30, I go into the kitchen and look in the ice box. Nothing tempts my palate. I have no appetite. There's a pad of eight-by-ten paper on the counter. I had started to write to one of the kids. I'd gotten as far as Dearest... something had distracted me and I'd never gotten back to it. I tear the top piece off the pad and fold it in half, the long way. I bend one end of the rectangle into triangles, then fold them back and crease them. I'm in my second childhood: making paper airplanes.

I carry my plane to the living room window. A scrap of candy wrapper floats by on the wind. It's blustery out there. There's a little footlocker under the window. I'd picked it up at a second hand store because it reminded me of my days in the army. I sit down on it and open the window. Leaning out, I shoot the plane into the breeze. It soars off, goes this way and that, and then plummets down toward the street. At the last minute, it doesn't crash, but turns and flies back up high. I give a little cheer. The wind begins to carry it east toward Central Park. The plane is gliding along at about a twelfth or thirteenth floor level. It's pretty far away by now, but there's still enough ambient light in the gloaming that I can make it out. It comes to the end of the block by the park, then disappears around the corner. I hang out the window trying to snag another look, but it's gone. I stand up. I'm restless, stir crazy, but I don't want to go out. There's a little seventeen inch TV on a coffee table in front of my Salvation Army sofa. I switch it on and channel surf for a while, then shut it off and shuffle into the john.

Back in the living room, I flop down on the couch and stare at the wall. Another night spent just waiting for nothing. After a bit, I head listlessly over to the window again and sit on the footlocker to check out the night. The sky is a pearly, luminescent pink, the high, white overcast clouds trapping the Manhattan neon and reflecting it back down to light up everything underneath. I glance over towards the park. A tiny pinpoint of white is in the distance, a little speck peeking around the corner of the building over at Central Park West. Flying at what seems to be a twenty five story level, it comes closer. It flits this way and that, then heads up in my direction. As it nears, I can feel my heart beating. The speck in the sky is starting to be recognizable. It's a paper airplane. I crane my neck for a better look. It's coming close. I am totally incredulous. I launched the plane a good fifteen minutes ago. Will it come near enough that I'll know for sure it's really mine?

It's flying toward me. This is crazy. There are more than a dozen buildings on my block. There are a hundred and eighty windows on the side of my building (I counted them the next day) and the plane is heading to the one I'm in. It's pointed right at me. I laugh out loud. The plane arrives. I reach out and pluck it from the air. The paper plane is mine. Dearest is written on the wing. What can this mean? What kind of crazy miracle is it? Send a paper airplane out of a thirty fourth story window and a quarter of an hour later it comes home to the same window? Once, I dreamed of being a virtuoso of the kazoo. What the hell is the point of a dumb miracle like this? The answer, the message, I tell myself, is that miracles do happen and will happen and are happening.

Needless to say, in a day or so, the fact that a miracle has taken place in my life, even a dumb one, recedes into the black hole of my unconscious and I'm back to my chosen line of work: staring catatonically at the wall. So God, utilizing Cotton Mather's stick with the knob on the end of it, bops me on the noggin again. It's evening. I'm sitting on my couch, trying to decide whether it's too early to go to bed. I glance up and whom do I see, standing in the hall between the kitchen and the living room but our Lord and Savior Jesus Christ. He doesn't say anything to me, just stands there in my hall, with the slightest trace of a smile on his face, radiating unconditional love. I recognize him at once. The experience is as real as any I've ever had in my life. I don't question it for an instant. I know the difference between real and imaginary. I'm a magician. Christ graces me with his presence for twenty minutes. Then I look away and when I turn back, he's gone. The next night, he comes again, standing in a different part of the room, visits for fifteen minutes or so, and then leaves. Oddly enough, I don't feel particularly changed by the experience. I just think to myself, "So, He's real and alive and living in New York."

A few days after later (belief in coincidence is a form of superstition), I receive word in the mail that the tenant in a cottage I own on the canals in Venice, California, is moving out. Back when my wife and I had migrated to the Golden State I had purchased a fine home in Pacific Palisades. Later, having discovered the run-down charms of Venice ("Where art meets crime"), I'd bought a small cottage there as well. In the divorce, she'd kept the manse, I'd held on to the little bungalow. It is now available for me to live in, so I decide to leave New York and move back out west. The kids are there, after all, and there is work in Hollywood.

XVIII

Venice, California 1983

In the early nineteen hundreds, Abbott Kinney, a wealthy American manufacturer, had traveled to Europe, visited Venice, Italy, marveled at it and said, "I want one." He returned home, moved to L.A. and bought up a large parcel of land near the beach. He hired city planners and announced that he would soon open a new community called Venice of America. He dug a big lagoon and scooped out a network of canals. He imported gondolas from Italy and gondoliers to operate them. He erected the largest roller coaster west of the Mississippi. He offered plots of land for sale on the canals. The project opened in 1905 with great fanfare. Kinney had bribed the city of L.A. into creating an electric railway from downtown so people could travel to the new Venice. He rented tents for two dollars a week so that even the poor could enjoy themselves. Charlie Chaplin built a summer home there, as did Clara Bow, the Marilyn Monroe of her day.

When I arrived at my cottage on the canals, I found, to my horror, that the tenant had painted the entire interior black: the walls, the doors, even the window frames! What the hell had been going on, devil worship? It took four coats of landlord white to cover the mess, but it gave me something to do. I settled in. Freshly painted, the cottage became quite livable. When I had paid $113,000 for it, all the locals had ragged on me. "You waited too long," they said. "You coulda got it for 75 grand last year. It's peaked now, you're screwed." It was small, with a living room, kitchen, bath and one bedroom. I hired a carpenter to add a second story with an extra bedroom and bath so the kids could sleep over. I had him construct a fireplace. The children started coming on weekends. Picking them up was awkward. I still ached for my wife. The marriage was over, but I couldn't accept it. I remembered a story I'd read as a young boy, in a long forgotten book:

It's the time of the Spanish Inquisition and a man is locked in a dungeon. He has been there for years and knows he will be there until he dies. The dungeon is deep under ground. The moss-covered walls are damp, his only companions the rats and scorpions that share his cell. Once a day a silent jailor unlocks his door and leaves him a tin plate with something filthy to eat. If he tries to speak to the jailor, he is struck. The prisoner has forgotten how many years he has been there. He has forgotten his anguish at the realization that he would never again see the sun or hear a bird sing or smell a flower or touch a woman or listen to the sound of a human voice.

Lately, the jailor has been drunk. Sometimes he hits the prisoner for no reason. Occasionally, he forgets to bring his food. One day, he throws a plate onto the slick floor of the cell, slams the door, and neglects to lock it. The prisoner's heart stops. He stands motionless, afraid to hope. After a while, he hears the sound of snoring. He pushes on the cell door. It moves slightly, making a grating sound. He freezes in terror, his mind racing wildly. The jailor continues to snore. The prisoner opens the door wide enough to slip out. Halfway down a long, dark hall, lit by a flickering torch, the jailor is asleep in a chair. A ring of keys hangs from his belt. The prisoner creeps slowly toward the sleeping jailor, sure that the beating of his heart will awaken him. He reaches for the keys. The jailor stirs. He freezes. Then, when the snoring resumes, he hooks a finger through the key ring and lifts it from the jailor's belt.

At the end of the hall is an iron door. The third key he tries fits and he finds himself at the bottom of steep, stone stairs. He is afraid he will collapse with excitement. Is it day or night outside? Will he see the sun or the stars? He climbs the steps and comes to another iron door. He chooses a key, it works, he pushes open the door and is free.

They are waiting for him. Two guards seize his arms. A Bishop of the Church steps from behind them. As the prisoner is being led back to his cell, he hears the sound of a human voice for the first and last time when the Bishop speaks to him.

"Without hope, my son, there can be no true despair."

My career had hit close to rock bottom. I was booked once in a while on dramatic TV programs and did the occasional appearance on a game show. But not much. I found myself making barely enough to pay my child support. I wasn't sure if I could come up with the modest mortgage payments on the cottage. Catatonia turned to terror. Was I through in the business? As if to confirm that dire prognosis, a period of two weeks went by in which my agent never called. I began to think of selling the house and moving into a furnished room. (The dramatic actor in me: not just a small apartment, but a furnished room.) That old demon Self Pity, something I had abhorred since childhood, began sinking its claws into me. I started downing a jigger of Irish whiskey every morning to "kick-start the day".

I turned on the tube one afternoon to watch the local five o'clock news. A band of homeless people had encamped themselves on the beach in Santa Monica, at the end of Rose Avenue. They had established a little community of houses made from packing crates and had become something of a tourist attraction. I decided to amble over and have a look. It was a fifteen minute walk. The group had occupied a spot on the sand next to the boardwalk, a promenade on which tourists strolled, gawking at the street entertainers, body builders and bikini babes for which Venice was famous. I positioned myself on the sidewalk with the out-of-towners, and watched. The homeless folk were having the time of their lives, enjoying being the center of attention. A channel two news truck was just leaving as I arrived. I focused on a guy standing in front of the refrigerator crate that was his home. He was frying sausages in a pan over a can of Sterno. He had, no doubt, cadged the money for these from the tourists. The sausages smelled delicious and the guy was whistling a happy little tune as he flipped them in his pan. It was five in the afternoon and the sun was sinking behind him, a thrillingly beautiful sunset. The guy seemed happy as a lark, not a care in the world, and had no mortgage to pay.

"Hmm," I thought. "This isn't bad. Maybe I should move over here and join them. A home on the beach without a mortgage, and every night a sunset." I began to mull the idea over sort of seriously. Then my ego went to work: "I could have the biggest box. I'd cut holes in it for windows and put up little curtains." I began to laugh at myself for the first time in weeks. When I arrived home at the cottage, there was a message on my answering machine. My agent had called with a voice-over gig. Then, I really started to laugh. I had stopped taking myself so seriously…and a job had appeared.

I recalled a time years before in New York, when I had gone to hear Reverend Ike, the great Prophet of Financial Plenty. His parishioners, he bragged, owned more Cadillac cars per capita than any other group in the country. "If you worry about the money," Reverend Ike had thundered in his church, "the money hears that and don't wanna come and play with you!" The congregation had howled with laughter. They had experienced that it was true. I decided on that late afternoon in Venice that the Reverend had been right, that I should stop worrying and revert to what I had been for most of my life: a devotee of the philosophy of Alfred E. Neuman.

I found a flier in my mailbox one morning. It announced that a man named Tolly Burkan would offer the experience of fire walking ("to overcome fear"). I had heard of him; he was a protégée of Tony Robbins, who had introduced the odd practice to this country, after stumbling across it in the Orient. The pamphlet said that if you sent in an advance payment of fifty bucks, they'd guarantee you a reservation, and that the event would take place on camp grounds in Pacific Palisades, not far from where I had lived with my family. Fire walking had never been on my list of anything to do, but as I was scared a lot of the time those days, I was willing to give it a try. As a kid, I had always wondered when the other shoe was going to drop (my father would leave and my mother would kill herself). Now, with my marriage dead and my career in shambles, the whole footwear store was closed. "I'll give it a shot," I told myself, and sent in the fifty bucks.

When the day arrived, I drove to the camp grounds, a twenty five minute trip. Forty of us would-be fakirs assembled in a rustic cabin on top of a hill, a short walk up from the parking lot where we had been instructed to leave our cars. The crowd was a mixed bag: aging hippies, students, business types. Thirty-two of the forty were men. The room was furnished with a semi-circle of wooden chairs with half desks attached to their right arms. It occurred to me that left handed people are usually out of luck when they need to take notes at a lecture.

Tolly Burkan, a solemn fellow, welcomed us and we filled out forms, including a promise not to sue if our feet got charred. I shuddered. Then we were instructed to march down the other side of the hill and participate in the building of the fire. A large pile of railroad ties had been brought in for the evening's festivities. Two of Tolly Burkan's assistants showed us how to stack them into a pyramid. When that was done, we backed off and the pyramid was doused with kerosene and lit. The fire blazed into the sky. It was 7:45 PM, a clear winter night, California cashmere weather. We then climbed back up to the cabin, took our seats, and waited for Burkan's talk to begin.

Once again, he welcomed us. It would take a couple of hours, he said, for the railroad ties to cook down to a bed of coals. While we waited for that to happen, white knuckled and nervous, Tolly Burkan gave his pitch. It was the usual New Age stuff: mind over matter ("I don't mind and you don't matter," a line from the lame comic MC at the nightclub in Lowell, Mass. popped into my mind).

"There are three rules you have to remember: Pay attention, Expect the best, and Go for it." I had heard variations on the theme before, but this time I was listening in a different context: I was going to walk on fire...or I was going to chicken out and not walk on fire. Either choice would be traumatic.

"People have been doing this for centuries," Tolly said. "And frankly, no one knows how or why it works." We were not there to learn the parlor trick of fire walking, he emphasized; letting go of arbitrary fear was our goal.

"And all fear," he explained, "is arbitrary. If you can overcome your apprehension tonight, the fire will not burn you. If you can't let go of fear, you dare not take the walk." The smell of incinerating railroad ties wafted through the window of our cabin. I was terrified.

"This is nuts. Why am I doing it?" I asked myself. But I knew the answer. I was so damned sick of feeling afraid. I knew I would have to let go of my fear, at least for that evening, if I was going to take the walk. And I was stubbornly determined to do so. I looked around, trying to detect from people's expressions whether they were going to walk or not. Some of them looked back at me and smiled nervously.

At 10:15, we trooped back down the hill. The night air was chillier now, but some of us were sweating. We approached the fire. It had burned down substantially. One of Burkan's assistants began giving us orders.

"Please take off your shoes and socks and roll up your pants if you are wearing them. Please do this whether you plan to take the walk or not." We obeyed obediently. ("You will be given bars of soap. Do not be alarmed; the room contains only showers.") As instructed, we found safe spots for our belongings, then joined hands, making a ring around the fire. Two more assistants appeared, with heavy rakes and pitchforks. They were wearing combat boots. Using the implements, they raked the dying bonfire into a path approximately four feet wide and nine feet long. We were standing a dozen feet away, and the heat was so intense I could barely stand it.

"This is lunacy," I thought. "It's cuckoo time. I've done a lot of crazy things in my life… blah, blah, blah." The roof chatter went on and on.

"The temperature in the fire is approximately 1100 degrees." Tolly Burkan had re-appeared and taken over. "Aluminum liquefies at this temperature and can be poured into castings." I glanced at the man whose right hand I was holding. He looked as frightened as I felt. "There is no shame in deciding not to take the walk. Remember the three rules. ONE. Pay attention. My assistants will walk first and you will see that they are not getting burned. TWO. Expect the best. Decide that you are going to accomplish what you intend to do. And finally, rule number THREE: Go for it. Step onto these coals and walk. Don't go too fast or you might trip and fall down. And whatever you do, don't stop. If you do, you will burn."

Burkan disappeared and there was a moment of silence. I stared down at the vivid swath a few yards away. The heat was intense. Flames were dancing around the glowing coals. Suddenly a man, one of Burkan's assistants, emerged from the ring of people, moved across the small buffer zone of grass, and stepped onto the red hot coal bed. I held my breath, watching him with fascination. His feet were sinking into the coals. Flames shot up around him. He took four or five steps across the length of the path and then he was off, stomping up and down in a damp patch of grass. My heart was pounding.

Now, another man walked into the inferno, and following him, a woman. She had on a dress, and clutched her skirt up around her thighs. People were now walking in a steady flow across the nine-foot length of fire. I saw it, I experienced it, I didn't believe it. "I can't do this," my ego screamed inside my head. "OK, pal," I answered back. "You stay here, I'm leaving." Suddenly, I was not afraid. I let go of my partner's hand and moved toward the fire. When an opening presented itself, I stepped onto the smoldering coals. The heat was intense. I felt the hardness of the burning embers under the soles of my feet, which had always been tender. I remembered that when I graduated from my Cub den to Boy Scout, I never rose above the rank of Tenderfoot. I looked down. Little tongues of flame were licking between my toes. As I took each step, disturbing the bed, dozens of tiny, broiling embers danced onto my feet.

I walked at a deliberate, moderately slow pace, determined not to rush the experience. Four steps, five…and then I was off on the cool grass, elated, victorious, my heart leaping for joy. My feet had not burned. There were still embers on them. I hopped up and down in the dewy grass, dislodging the burning remnants. I couldn't keep the grin off my face. Fellow walkers were pumping my hand and congratulating me. By the end of he fire walk, 31 of the 40 enrollees had taken the trip. There was a euphoria among them. People were clapping one another on the back. I spotted one of the men who hadn't walked. He seemed to be trying to keep up a good front. I heard him say to one of the other non-walkers, "I really just came to observe."

The next day, as fate would have it, I was booked on one of my infrequent TV appearances, a game show called Super Password. I found myself in the Big Money Bonus Round, sitting across from an excited contestant. I had 60 seconds to come up with clues to help her find ten secret words. If I was able to do so, she would win $45,000. With the prize money that high, tension inevitably mounted. I reminded myself to PAY ATTENTION (to the words for which I had to find clues…and to my partner's responses). EXPECT THE BEST (this really is an easy game if the players are relaxed), and GO FOR IT (the buzzer sounded). Effortlessly, one after another, I gave the right clues. Thirty three seconds later, the contestant was screaming, jumping up and down, and hugging me and the host of the show. I drove home after the taping, elated, firmly believing that my fear had gone away forever.

I was, as usual, wrong.

XIX

My morning jigger of Irish whiskey expanded to include a five o'clock cocktail and a bottle of wine. Before I knew it, I was "well into the cooking sherry" on a regular basis. One morning a neighbor, whose name I can't remember (but I thank him), dropped by the house and said to me, "You seem to be getting pretty tanked these days. Why don't you come to one of my meetings? There's one just up the way on Wilshire, and it starts in an hour." I told him I'd be happy to go check it out, though there was no way I was an alcoholic.

It was wonderful: a stag meeting, populated by of a bunch of guys who smiled, pumped my hand and seemed genuinely glad to see me. There were thirty five or forty of them, mostly white, middle class men. The get-together took place three afternoons a week in the back room of a restaurant called Papa John's. There was a table set up in a semi-circle and everybody ate lunch and took turns speaking.

"My name is Joe, and I'm an alcoholic."

"Hi Joe."

When my turn came (the boy who'd put coal dust on his forehead on Ash Wednesday), I didn't want to seem different. So I said, "My name is Orson, and I guess I'm an alcoholic." There was laughter all around and I gave my little spiel. I don't remember what I said but it went over well and I was invited to go to another meeting that evening. The general theme at the meetings had to do with turning one's life over to a "higher power." That sounded like God, which made me nervous; the last thing I wanted to do was get involved with a religious organization. Jesus had come to visit me and all, but that was personal. Organized anything tended to turn me off. But I was assured that my higher power could be the ocean, or a tree, or a doorknob, anything other than myself. When I felt like taking a drink, I should call on my higher power. And if that didn't work, I should call one of the guys. Several of them gave me their phone numbers and offered to "sponsor" me.

It all seemed harmless enough, and I stopped drinking at once and began attending meetings every day at different locations around town, some of them in churches, some in donated halls. At most of the meetings, there was a speaker who "shared" his experience, after which whoever wanted to do so spoke up about problems he was having with the booze. A basket was passed around and everyone would stick a dollar in it to defray the cost of the coffee and donuts, which were offered at each meeting. No one seemed to be in charge, yet each meeting went off without a hitch.

Occasionally, a speaker would wax spiritual and tell about how his life had changed for the better because of his relationship with God. No one seemed to object to this, and the talks never became preachy. One speaker told a joke: St. Peter is giving a newcomer a tour of heaven. He opens a door and points to a solemn looking group of worshippers. He says, "These are our Baptists." He opens another door and people are counting Rosary beads. He says, "These are our Catholics." When he opens the third door, cigarette smoke pours out (alcoholics all smoked in those days) accompanied by gales of laughter.

"Who are these?" asks the newcomer.

"We don't know," says St. Peter. "And they won't tell us."

Four weeks into it, I heard a speaker who impressed the hell out of me. It was at a 6:45 A.M. meeting I had begun to attend regularly. I had volunteered to get up at five in the morning twice a week, pick up the donuts and make the coffee. The speaker's name was Frankie. That's how he introduced himself and we yelled back, "Hi Frankie."

Frankie was not shy about telling his story. A tough looking guy with a tattoo on his neck, he'd done time in the pen. Hard time. The last time he was arrested, he was taken off the roof of a building in downtown L.A. by a SWAT team; helicopters, the whole shebang. They sent him away for fifteen years for something pretty violent, I'm sure; he didn't say. It was his third conviction but this was before three strikes, so he didn't get life.

Well while he was up the river, he started going to meetings. To break up the monotony, I suppose. And somehow or other, he got the message and his whole life turned around. While he was still there in the joint, he began helping other cons and staying out of trouble, and they knocked some time off his sentence. By the time I came across him, he was out, of course, and working at a regular job, going to meetings, and sponsoring a number of young men. "My babies," he called them.

Frankie fascinated me. His mug was rough, but his eyes were filled with inner peace. I decided I had to talk to him. When the meeting was over, I found him outside on the pavement. A cute young thing was bending his ear and he was obviously enjoying it. There were a few of us waiting around, wanting to grab a moment with him, but of course we all understood that if a good looking girl was praising him, probably flirting with him, manners and common sense dictated that we wait our turn.

The young woman finished and started to leave, but before any of us could get a shot at him, a strange thing happened. An L.A.P.D. motorcycle cop drove by on his big, black Harley, spotted Frankie, jammed on the brakes, jumped off the bike, ran over and grabbed hold of him. Holy God, we all thought, he's done something bad again and they've come to get him. But instead of arresting him, the cop gave him a big hug. Then he got back on the Harley and blasted off. Frankie turned to the little group of us there on the sidewalk.

"One of my babies," he explained, and started down the street. I decided to be a pain in the neck and hustled after him. I caught up and introduced myself. I told him about my reluctance to think of my higher power as anything divine. What advice did he have, I asked.

"Get down on your knees," he said, "and thank God every morning. Do it again at night."

"But I don't know if I believe in God."

"It doesn't matter. Just do it."

"Why do I have to get on my knees?"

"He likes it."

And that was all he said. He stood there looking at me for a minute, and then I thanked him and he took off. I got into the little Chevy Sprint I was driving and returned to my cottage. I made a cup of coffee, carried it out onto my porch that overlooked the canal, and sat down on a broken wicker chair. I had obviously been flirting with the idea of some kind of a Supreme Being for a long time now. Why was I resisting? Was I worried about what my friends would think? I didn't have any friends. And all my new acquaintances were very much into the idea of a higher power.

I decided that all else having failed, I would follow the instructions. That night, I brushed my teeth and got undressed as usual, ready to retire. My bedroom was Spartan, furnished with only a mattress and box spring, and the small footlocker I'd carried out from New York. The locker had a reading lamp on it. Beside it was a 5x7 picture of Jesus. I didn't necessarily believe in his divinity, but since he had called on me in Manhattan, I felt sort of a connection with him.

I had purchased the picture, a reproduction of a painting by Hofmann, at The Self Realization Center in the Palisades. Monks of some kind lived there. They wore orange robes. Sunday services, open to the public, were held in the chapel. The grounds were beautiful and contained a lovely little lake. On the chapel's altar stood a photograph of Gandhi and paintings of the avatars of all the great religions, including a larger version of the one I had of Jesus. I attended a few of these services, but found no particular inspiration in their one-size-fits-all approach to matters spiritual. When I walked into the Self Realization gift shop and picked up Jesus' picture, the clerk gave me a friendly little tip. One of the Center's monks, he said, had been incarnated in the Holy Land back when Christ was around, and had assured him that the painting was a very good likeness.

In my bedroom that night, I got down on my knees, folded my hands, glanced at the picture of Jesus, and then said aloud, "If there's anybody there, thank you for my day." Not being able to think of anything to add to my prayer, I climbed into bed, switched off the lamp, and quite quickly fell asleep. When I woke up in the morning, I got back down on my knees beside the bed and said, once again out loud, "If there's anybody there, thank you for my night's sleep." Then I took a shower, got dressed, ate a bowl of Frosted Flakes, and went about my business. It wasn't one of my early-riser-pick-up-the-donuts days, but I did go to a meeting later on. I told no one of my new morning and evening regime, but thought about it on and off throughout the afternoon. I was torn. Part of me felt stupid and was glad the kids hadn't slept over, seen me kneeling at the bed, and thought to themselves, "What weird stuff is dad into now?" Another part of me felt, for reasons I couldn't understand, kind of excited.

I doggedly continued to say my little prayer morning and night for weeks, and without my even being aware of it, it stopped feeling foolish to me. It started feeling good, in fact. After a while, I began to feel as if my little thank you prayers were being heard. I didn't know by whom or by what, but it was a good feeling. Then, before I knew it, I felt as if there was something or someone there who knew me and cared about me. Actually loved me. Alright, I told myself, I'll use the G word. "Thank you, God," I whispered one morning. And I meant it. And that's how I became a believer. As simple as that. No ritual, no dogma. Just a repeated little mantra which I came to mean.

My life progressed. Kids sleeping over on weekends, coffee with my buddies from the program. No women. I had decided that I was going to take as long as it took to understand why I had done what I had done to screw up my marriage, and not do anything like that again. I knew that I had to learn to be completely self sufficient, at least in any romantic sense. I would stay celibate until my new pal God whispered in my ear that I was ready, and sent me the right one. If that was never, it would have to be okay.

Back in Cambridge, George had broken up with Isobel Hickey. I had gone to visit him from time to time, usually bringing the kids with me. I wanted them to be able to have the relationship with their grandfather which I'd never achieved. He was quite sweet with them and they really came to care for him. Margaret Mead once said that the reason grandparents and their grandchildren get along is that they have a common enemy. He always attracted women, old retired school teachers, mostly, who took turns looking after him. I got to know some of them over the years because they wrote me letters. He used them to say things he wouldn't say himself. "Your father was so proud when you got good reviews in that show at the Shubert." He'd never tell me himself, of course. Or, "Your father feels so bad when you don't come to see him. He's getting frail and really shouldn't be left alone."

There was a message on my answering machine when I came back from a week out of town. It was from the old dame of the day, saying that my father was in the Mt. Auburn Hospital. I called right away and it turned out he'd just been released and was on his way home. He was eighty-three by then. He'd had a fall and had trouble getting up from the sidewalk. When they examined him, they found out he was undernourished. I phoned the lady who'd left the message and she gave me her pitch, said that he doesn't bother to eat when he's home alone. He has enough money, she said, but just won't take responsibility for himself. "He gets the Meals on Wheels three times a week but doesn't even open the containers. When I'm over there, I put the food out on the table and make him sit down and eat it. Then, he has a perfectly good appetite. But when he's alone, he just won't. It's like he'd rather die than take responsibility for himself." The old lady seemed pretty smart.

Anyway, by the time I got the message, he'd spent a few days in the hospital and they'd fattened him up. He loved the attention from the doctors and nurses, and the old school teachers had taken turns going to see him. They managed to work it out, apparently, so that they were never there at the same time. Sort of a revolving, geriatric harem. He'd eaten the place out of house and home, even asked for seconds on Jello. But by now, he was back home and who knew what was going to happen? A few days later, I got a letter from the woman who'd left the phone message. She said she was in her eighties and not as strong as she used to be. "I get over to your father's place as often as I can. He's not well enough to be left alone and doesn't understand his financial situation."

So now I had a real guilt trip laid on me. I decided I had to fly back east and see what I could do for him. I didn't want to make the trip, but I had God whispering in my ear now. One of the inconveniences of becoming a believer. I called my father and told him I'd come in and spend a few days helping him get his act together, his banking affairs and all. He was delighted and said he'd get all the paperwork ready. I took the red eye to Logan and cabbed it to Harvard Square. He had moved to a somewhat larger apartment a few blocks from the one I'd shared with him. It was on Plimpton Street, just off Mass. Avenue, more former student housing the university had found for him.

The place was pretty much of a mess, boxes of papers and periodicals. He had letters he hadn't answered since the fifties, which he wouldn't throw away. He seemed to hold onto everything on the grounds that he might need it some day. I reached into one of the boxes and came up with a magazine from 1937. Not even an interesting magazine. I asked him if there was an article in it he was saving, or what? He said no, so I went to heave it in the trash can. He practically jumped out of his skin. "No, gimme that. There must have been some reason I kept it!" And dust flew as he went through boxes looking for other stuff he must have kept for some reason. I asked him if he'd dug out the papers we'd talked about on the phone, the bank statements and all. So we could figure out his financial situation.

"They're around here somewhere," he said. "It's okay. I'm in good shape. Don't worry about it." And he changed the subject and started complaining about one of his girlfriends.

"Wait a minute," I interrupted. "I flew here to help you with this stuff, and you said you'd have it ready. What about those investments the lawyer made for you?" He'd told me that some shyster had gotten him twenty five grand when he'd been in an auto accident, and had put it into bonds or something for him.

"Oh, I don't know where those papers are right now but it's alright. The lawyer is trustworthy."

"Well, what's his name?"

"Whose name?"

"The lawyer, George."

"Oh, hell, I don't remember. It's probably in my phone book somewhere." But of course we couldn't find the phone book in the endless boxes of 1937 magazines. So it turned out there wasn't a damn thing I could do for him after flying all the way across the country.

I took him out to lunch at a Chinese restaurant, and he ate like a wart hog, polishing off all of his food and half of mine; and that night, we dined Italian. I slept on the couch in his front room, breathing dust. The next day I took him out for one last meal, and then I flew home, picturing his face from time to time on the way back. It wore the same expression I had seen when he told his suicidal wife he was going to Alaska, and would be leaving a sixteen year old boy to look after her.

I knew the day was going to come when I'd get a call from some hospital to say that my father was too feeble and disoriented to go home and what would I like them to do with him? What the hell was I going to say? He was too stubborn to let me do anything for him, but at the same time he acted helpless and wanted me to take over. By the time I got back to L.A. I was really fuming. I went to the meeting where I'd first been introduced to the program, the one in the back room of Papa John's.

When it came my turn to share, I told the guys about what I'd gone through and how angry and frustrated I was. There was a long pause when I finished sharing and, of course, that annoyed the hell out of me. The next guy who spoke said that he hoped his program had taught him to be more open and loving to his family than I seemed to be. I felt like walking out of the meeting. But then one of the alcoholics spoke up. A guy named Marshall, who wore a Dodgers baseball cap. He looked at me.

"Hey, pal. You're worrying about something that hasn't happened yet. When the phone rings, God will let you know what to do." The moment he said it, I relaxed.

When the meeting was over, I drove home, made a cup of coffee, carried it out onto the porch, and sat down on my broken wicker chair. I had a lot to digest. When Marshall had spoken, I was sure that he'd been right, that God would provide me with the answer when I needed it. But how could I really know that? Slowly and surely the old, familiar doubt sank its fangs into me. What proof was there that God existed? And if he did, why would he get involved in my life? Or anybody's life? Was my new belief just an example of ignorance being bliss? If it was, I didn't want to go back to the folly of being wise. But what choice did I have if God is only a myth to keep us from feeling lost in a cold, cruel world? Sitting in the broken wicker chair, my morning and evening prayers forgotten, I was suddenly filled with despair.

On impulse, I stormed out of the cottage, jumped in my Chevy Sprint and drove to Barnes and Noble on the mall in Santa Monica, hoping to find proof of a Creator there.

"Lord, if you exist, find me a way to be sure," I prayed aloud. I parked the Sprint at a meter, threw a quarter into the slot, walked to the store, and rode the escalator up to the sections called Religion and Science. Half an hour later, I was on my way home with a small stack of books. Then back to my wicker chair with fresh coffee and my stash. Two of the tomes, written by apparently non-believing cosmologists, had the temerity to suggest that earth (our puny little planet in a pint-sized solar system on the edge of a not particularly significant galaxy) may actually be the only place in the universe where intelligent life exists. Ridiculous? Well, nature is profligate. I had wasted billions of sperm in my lifetime (though not lately) to come up with four kids.

In a paperback called *The Hidden Face of God*, an M.I.T.-trained physicist offered what he claimed to be scientific evidence of the overwhelming probability of God's existence. For the universe to have come about by accident, he wrote, the number of coincidences required was unimaginable. (One of the books I'd seen on the shelf and not bought at Barnes and Noble was titled *It Takes a Lot of Faith to be an Atheist*.) *Hidden Face of God* was heavy going. I sat on my wicker chair and read. And read. I read until my eyes glazed over and went out of focus. Then I rested a bit and read some more. Days later I finished.

Then, obsessed, I went back and slogged through it all over again. Done at last, I sat and cogitated (one of my grandfather's words).

Cosmologists have calculated the age of the universe. I hadn't known that, back then. The Hubble telescope showed that all the stars are running away from one another. The expanding universe, they called it. So the scientists figured out how fast they were traveling, reversed it, did the math, and found out when the trip began. A little pinpoint of something or other had exploded (the Big Bang) and a few seconds later, all the ingredients needed to whip up the entire cosmos had appeared.

Galaxies formed, came apart, then re-formed. Eons later, one of these became our 'hood, the Milky Way, not a heavy hitter as galaxies go. And in the boondocks of the Milky Way, not in the center city where the action is, but off in the sticks near the edge (ideally situated, actually, without all that ambient starlight, for the Hubble to be able to photograph distant nebulae) was our little star. And spinning around it were nine planets.

Earth is exactly the right distance from its star; a bit closer and we'd burn, a tad farther away and we'd freeze. We have the moon we need for there to be life on earth, and it's just the right distance from us. If it were a little farther away or a little closer, or a little bigger or a little smaller, the earth would either be nothing but ocean or dry as a bone. We have just the right amount of water, which we keep recycling. A drunk chugs a six pack and takes a wiz in the bushes. The sun soaks it up and the next day, purified, it comes back as rain. Maybe I took a shower this morning in the exact same water Moses waded into when he parted the Red Sea. There are deserts, of course, but they wouldn't be a problem if it weren't for us humans. The nomads in North Africa used to pack up and move on when the rain stopped and everything went dry. When it started raining again, they came back. They liked it that way, the way circus people like going on the road. But when the Europeans came and stuck up arbitrary borders, the nomad people were screwed. They had to stay put where there wasn't any water and wait for Care packages.

We worry about global warming; the ice caps will melt. In the fifties, Rachel Carson wrote a book called *The Sea Around Us*. I had a copy of it. She said New York City would be under water in twenty years. In the eighties, Newsweek had a cover story about the approaching ice age. We are worrywarts. It's our nature.

Einstein proved that there isn't any matter. Nothing is solid. It's all just energy that looks and feels real. The new quantum physics and molecular biology people are finding out incredible stuff. The steel in the Chrysler Building is made of atoms that are 99.999999999 empty. Some far out quantum physicists think that even that final .01 is not there. It's all energy. And the smart boys are starting to believe that the energy is made up of information. (God's ideas?) We're literally living in the information age. The human body is complex and brilliant. Every little atom has a job to do and knows how to do it, every gene. There's wisdom in every cell of our body.

My kids were growing up, starting to marry and have kids of their own. One of them had a baby at St. John's in Santa Monica. While I was in the room holding on to my beautiful grand-daughter, the nurse in charge of teaching new mothers how to breast feed came in and told us an astonishing thing. When a mother kisses her newborn baby, she inhales its breath. The baby's breath contains all the information about what the baby needs. So the mother's milk adapts to fill the baby's needs. Every mother's milk is a just a bit different from every other. They've done tests at St. John's that show this. Every gene in our body has a function and knows how to do it.

So, who put all of this together? Who drew up the plans for the gorgeous world we live in and the light show we call the cosmos? The world of academe claims to rely on science, but won't ask the hard question: what (if not God) existed before the Big Bang? At a convention in Chicago a group of scholars, determined to prove that life came about on its own through nothing but evolution, hired some math geniuses and asked them to figure out how many billion years it would have taken for the first little amoeba to evolve into a human being. The math guys went to work and came back with their answer. The earth wasn't old enough, they said, so it couldn't have happened that way. The scholars said well it did happen that way so your math must be wrong.

Alright. We can't prove for sure that God exists or doesn't, but there's enough circumstantial evidence to convict any guest star on Law and Order. So I'll stop fighting it. You the man, God.

As for Jesus being the His Son? I dunno, ya know? I'd need more time in the wicker chair.

———•———

In the course of my studies I learned something I didn't want to know: ten percent of the gross weight of every living thing on earth is ants.

XX

L.A. 1992

Twelve years after my divorce, God gave me another shot at love. I had been asked to take part in a staged script reading in Hollywood. Dan Lauria was producing a series of them to help fledgling screenwriters. I knew of him; he played the husband on a TV series called The Wonder Years. It was one of the few shows I watched on the tube. My oldest son was addicted to it and when he went off to spend a sabbatical in France with his high school group, he begged me to record every episode so he could watch them when he got home. I thought that Alley Mills, the actress who played the wife, was a fox. And when the reading took place in an old movie theater on La Cienega Boulevard, there in the front row sat the fox; Lauria had invited her. My heart skipped a beat (and you thought I wasn't a writer). I hadn't dated since my divorce, figured I'd remain a bachelor for the rest of my days. But there sat the fox.

After the reading, the half dozen members of the cast were invited to a nearby restaurant for a drink and a bite. Alley's (great looking) mother was in town for a few days to help her daughter move into a new house she had just bought. She had come to the reading, and it was she who had extended the invitation. We strolled up the block and into the restaurant where we were seated at a large round table. I grabbed the chair between Alley and her mother and spent equal time chatting with both of them. I wondered if the old lady thought I was hitting on her. I learned that mom would be returning home to Connecticut the next afternoon. Summoning up the courage, I asked Ms Mills, as casually as I could, if she would consider having dinner with me. She said she'd be pleased to do so, and gave me her phone number.

On the appointed evening, I showed up at her fine big new house in Hancock Park, wearing a necktie and carrying flowers. Looking back, I realize I must have seemed ridiculously old fashioned and formal. I had reserved a table at a suitably impressive eatery, a fancy place called Maple Drive. The kitchen was run by Leonard Schwartz, one of a new chefs who were bringing comfort food back into fashion We drove to the restaurant where we ate meatloaf and mashed potatoes (Leonard's specialty), and talked. And talked and talked. For hours. I found everything she had to say fascinating. I was smitten.

Alley was forty and had never been married. (I ventured into that cage with a chair, whip and blank cartridge.) She had lived for years in a sweet little cottage in West Hollywood, not unlike mine on the canal. Having finally made some dough on The Wonder Years, she had decided it was time to buy herself a big house, where she could entertain her friends. She had, as it turned out, closed on the place, on Cherokee Street, a tree lined thoroughfare, the day before we met. Her mother had flown out from New Haven (where she lived with her husband, the publisher of The Yale Press) to help her daughter move in.

Alley's background, and true love, was in theater. She had apprenticed at Williamstown, graduated (magna cum laude, I learned subsequently) from the first class of women at Yale, where she studied acting, along with Meryl Streep, Sigourney Weaver, and a slew of aspiring young actors, many of whom went on to be successful in the business. She then moved to London to get her Masters in performing arts at the London Academy of Music and Dramatic Arts. (I told her I had barely squeaked through high school.) Her first Equity job was on a cross-country tour playing Juliet. The tour ended in Hollywood where she got cast in a play, then became sidetracked with the offer of a TV series and had remained in that medium.

Alley was a Buddhist, had been active in that practice for years. She had made numerous trips to Japan and had acted as a mentor of sorts to scores of young women. I told her I wasn't sure what I was, but that I believed in God.

"Buddhists believe in a universal Law," she said. "It's pretty much the same thing."

"No it isn't. In Buddhism, there's no one to feel grateful to."

"You can feel grateful to the Law."

"How do you feel grateful to a law?"

And so it went. But we hit it off. I was nuts about her.

I began a courtship. It was hard. I was twenty three-years older than Alley. She'd had a succession of relationships with men who treated her badly. She had complained to a shrink about the guys in her life and he'd said, "You're picking them, you know." She was determined to change her taste in men, but wasn't finding it easy. When she saw that I was serious, she became wary. And blunt.

"You're too old. You'll make me fall in love with you and then you're going to die."

"What are you worried about? The new guy will take you to the funeral."

We started going to movies. Dating. Like a couple. We saw *Francis Ford Coppolla's Dracula*. Afterwards, walking to the car, she said. "I liked the picture, but what was it really about?"

"He's six hundred," I told her, "she's eighteen...and it works out."

I was determined to have her, even if it only lasted a year, which I was afraid it might. It would be worth a heart re-broken to have that year. A few months went by. I suspected (hoped) she was starting to cave. I went to the May Company and bought a ring. After dinner at a pizzeria one night, I dropped the little box with the ring in it on the table in front of her.

"This is for you," I said. "You can keep it and wear it, or give it back, or throw it away." She looked down at the box for a while, then opened it and tears came into her eyes. She took out the ring and held it up to the light.

"It's beautiful," she said. "Just beautiful.'

"It's from the May Company."

"Oh," she said, and laughed. She looked at it a while longer.

"I don't know, Ors'. I'm pretty scared."

I didn't say anything. She looked at the ring some more. Then she put it back in the box and closed it. I was afraid she was going to hand it back to me, but she didn't. She opened her purse and dropped the box in.

"Let me think about it, okay?"

I nodded. At least she'd held on to it.

A month later, on Christmas Eve when we exchanged presents, she handed me a box from Brooks Brothers. There was a grey cashmere sweater in it. When I took the sweater from the box, a little white card fell out. I picked it up. It had a single work written on it. Yes. I gasped with joy. Tears of happiness filled my eyes. I took her in my arms. "I promise to make you happy," I said. "When can we get married?"

She laughed. "Give me a minute."

"Next month?"

"What if I want to be a June bride?"

"I'm old. You keep pointing that out. I don't want to wait that long." I felt like singing The September Song.

"How about May? I have to find a dress. Everything."

"April."

"Alright, alright. Wow, you're stubborn."

"I'm in love."

———•◦•———

We celebrated the wedding in Alley's big new house in Hancock Park. A Jesuit priest I had befriended on the program officiated. Since neither of us was Catholic, his bishop had told him he could conduct the ceremony but the license would have to be signed by somebody else. Another friend of mine from the program had become a mail-order minister to avoid going to Viet Nam. He provided the legal form. The night before the wedding, Alley, per tradition, remained apart from the groom in the new house with her mother who had flown back out for the occasion, and her sister who was married to the top editor at Random House. I stayed home in Venice and tried to keep the grin off my face.

Alley's brother, a musician, flew in from Oakland and sang at the ceremony. As he did, the bride walked down the stairs on her father's arm. Tears came into my eyes once more. I had never seen anyone so beautiful. Half the guests were Alley's Buddhists and the other half my people from the program. And of course, my kids. And Fred Savage and Dan Lauria from The Wonder Years. My Jesuit priest friend made reference in the service to Buddhism and to Christianity. As part of the ceremony, we toasted each other with ersatz wine. I spilled some on myself. The wedding guests laughed. I said, "My cup runneth over... and staineth my shirt." Leonard Schwartz catered; we dined on meatloaf and mashed potatoes.

We spent a one-night honeymoon at a hotel on the beach in Malibu and then I had to go to work on a series I had just been cast in, *Dr. Quinn, Medicine Woman*. My career, like my love life, had become rejuvenated. We spent the first six months of our marriage commuting between Alleys new house in Hancock Park, where we spent weekdays, and my cottage on the canals where we relaxed on Saturdays and Sundays. I knew that her place was too fancy for her, but had to be patient till she realized it herself. When she finally got sick of the commute and decided to sell the house on Cherokee, it was her idea. In Venice, I had bought the cottage next to mine; we connected the two buildings with a greenhouse-style walkway, and together they became a home for us and Alleys cat, Kisha. We hired a contractor to take the interior walls and ceilings out of the new cottage. He held the walls together with thin steel rods and toggle bolts. This secured the roof (no two-by-fours needed), and the house became one big, airy room: our kitchen/dining area. We had plank floors installed, and the walls painted white. The bedrooms (and baths) were in the original cottage, with French doors looking out on the yard.

On Main Street in Santa Monica we discovered "The Australian Trading Company (Hand Made Furniture and Carpentry)." It was run by a pair of good-looking young sisters from Down Under. One did the construction, the other handled sales. In their shop, we found an old, seven-foot long work bench with built-in drawers; it was made of antique barn wood. We bought it and had the girls install it in the center of our new kitchen. We asked if they could design furniture to go around it. They could and did, adding an extension to the counter to hold our stovetop and oven, and a marble-top structure for the sink. Everything was made of old barn wood, as were the wall cabinets they built and hung.

This clean and open space became our primary living area. We furnished it with a big old rough-hewn French table from the 1700s, which Alley had owned forever, church pews of mine to go on either side of it, a wicker couch, coffee tables, an old porch glider, and antiques from a local dealer. A six foot wide, gilded antique mirror hung at the end of the table, and paintings by local Venice artists covered the rest of the walls. We added a grand piano, on which, when we were alone in the evenings, Alley played while I sang show tunes.

The front of the cottage gave onto a good-sized deck, which bordered the canal. The back wall consisted of a glass door and windows through which we looked at a wide expanse of grass with a beautiful fig tree in it. Alley, possessed of a green thumb, planted roses and wild flowers which grew, over time, into a riot of color. And as if our expanse were not enough, yet a third cottage became available next to ours. Alley bought it with the money from the sale of the house she'd purchased the day before she met me. Now we had a guest house for her mother to come visit.

XXI

My job on *Dr. Quinn, Medicine Woman*, stretched into a six year run. Jane Seymour was the star; I played Loren Bray, the crusty old man who owned the town's general store. Jim Knobeloch played the local barber; he became my buddy. The series was shot in the mountains above Malibu, thrillingly beautiful country. When guest directors were hired to shoot an episode, they would gaze at the scenery in the early morning and take their time plotting beautiful pictures. But because the sun set behind the mountains by late afternoon, the days were short (particularly in winter). In danger of losing the light, the directors would frantically try to wind up with something, *anything* in the can.

"Get that shot and print it!" they'd cry. Standing beside me during one of these frenzied moments, Jim whispered in my ear, "Gone With The Wind in the morning...Dukes Of Hazard at night."

The show took a break (and The Wonder Years had finished airing) so we had time at last for a proper honeymoon. We flew to Italy, starting our trip in the city ours was named after. When the concierge at the Danieli inspected our passports and saw that we were from Venice of America, he upgraded us to the honeymoon suite on the Grand Canal. From Venice we traveled by rent-a-car to Florence to take a look at Michaelangelo's David. We didn't stay long in Florence, nothing there for us after seeing the astonishing David. Then on to Sienna, a medieval walled city famous for the Duomo and great outdoor pizza joints, where musicians played till two A.M., and little kids ran around late at night making that sound that bands of kids make in Italian movies.

We hit the northwest coast where the tour books tell you not to go because there's nothing of interest there. The highway to the beach was lined with working class camp sites and trailers. We checked into a cheap motel, then walked into town and devoured mouth-watering grilled shrimp at a sidewalk cafe. No tourists came near the area, so none of the locals spoke English, but everyone was friendly and we made out fine with sign language and our smattering of Italian ("Il conte, per piacere. Grazie.).

Posters on walls announced that a traveling Italian circus was in town. They depicted Kirste the lion tamer, a hot-looking blonde in a bikini, who wielded her whip on a dozen ferocious cats. I managed to shop-lift a poster off the wall of the cafe, rolled it up and hid it under my jacket. We went to the circus that night. Kirste was a fat guy in a green suit, and both lions were toothless and sleepy. We had a great time.

As we were leaving the tent at the end of the performance, a teenaged girl from the circus family (we had seen her on the trapeze) raced after us, calling out to Alley, "Wonder Years? Wonder Years?" The family, it seemed, had played Las Vegas, and the girl had practiced English watching re-runs of Alley's show. We were invited to the family trailer (the largest of any circus family in all of Italy, they bragged), served espresso and introduced to the cast of the circus, all related. The girl translated, explaining that we were actors from America. I asked the fat guy in the green suit what had happened to Kirste. He gave me a look. "Uh, she's busy," he said. (I was in the business; I should understand about the poster.)

Next, we drove to Rome and after that to the glorious Amalfi coast with its crystal clear water. Then, on to the ruins of Pompeii, where I slipped a guide a twenty to take us into a not-open-to-the-public private house where well-to-do Pompeiians had lived with twenty servants per family member. You have a little more, you live a little better. From Italy we flew to Zermat, Switzerland where, I guess to prove to Alley that I wasn't such an old guy after all, we went parasailing off the mountain across from the Matterhorn. Almost three miles in the air, and held up by thirty two ounces of parachute silk. Practically as much fun as walking on fire. Then, the honeymoon over, home and back to work. I had more years to go on Dr. Quinn; Alley was hired to recur on the show as Jane Seymour's aristocratic sister from Boston.

On the family front, my oldest daughter, living in Paris, had fallen in love with and married a young Frenchman. (Alley and I flew over for the wedding). A few years after their second child was born, he decided he wanted to move to America and live near his wife's people. The canal house next to our three was on the market, so they bought it, giving the family four cottages in a row. (Like the Kennedys, we had a compound.) Before leaving France, they asked us to look for pre-schools in the neighborhood. The first one we saw was run by a Lutheran church a few blocks away. The school looked good, but we thought we had better check the place out to see how much Jesus they were going to lay on the kids (my son-in-law was a Jewish agnostic).

It turned out there had been a fire in the church, so services were being held pro tem in the Parish hall. When we entered the room, tears came into Alley's eyes. There was a portrait of Jesus on the wall. It was identical to the one which had sat on the bedside table of the Black woman who had raised and loved her when her mother had been off at work. Mary had held little Alley on her lap and read to her from the bible for years, until her unbelieving father had found out and angrily forbidden it. Alley looked at the picture, thought of Mary and all that she had taught her. She was deeply moved.

When the service began, we were so taken with the pastor, Ken Frese, that we started attending church every Sunday. Alley kept thinking of her dear Mary. She told the preacher that she was a Buddhist, "but might it be alright," she asked one Sunday "if I took communion?" He said he'd make an exception "if you'll agree to have coffee with me once a week."

And that's how Alley became a Christian. That, and Mary's picture of Jesus.

(I was a tougher nut to crack.)

Going to church and finding genuinely warm and friendly people in the pews around me diminished some of my prejudice against organized religion. (Not that the place was particularly organized; the service invariably started five or ten minutes late.) I liked singing the old hymns, which I remembered from my grandparents' church in Vermont. The dogma put me off, but I tried to keep an open mind. I started having coffee with Pastor Ken, and he went to work on my resistance to Jesus' being the Son of God.

"God is not just about love," said the preacher one morning over his buttered bagel. "He's a God of justice, too. Bad behavior has to be paid for, in this life or the next. We all have guilty consciences and usually deserve them. Tell me you don't get nervous when there's a cop car cruising behind you." I wasn't going to

"Look at history. We humans have acted fairly despicably, right from the beginning. Two thousand years ago, God might well have had enough, and been tempted to call an end to the whole thing, like he did once before with the Flood. Instead, he chose to be merciful and pay the price Himself, by taking on human form and enduring a terrible punishment on our behalf. If we accept the gift he offered," said Pastor Ken, "we're forgiven and get to make a fresh start."

Jesus as whipping boy. It was a lot to digest, and I didn't claim to understand it. But I don't understand why the bulb lights up when I flick the switch.

"The miracles are hard for me to swallow," I told the preacher one day.

"The definition of a miracle," he said, "is something that violates accepted scientific law. Atheists don't realize it, but they're into miracles just as much as we Christians are. They say the universe just *appeared* somehow. Science doesn't buy that. It contradicts the First Law of Thermodynamics ("Matter and energy will not emerge from a vacuum"). Atheists claim life just grew on its own out of inert matter. The Law of Bio-genesis says uh-uh… only in a Frankenstein movie. Everybody has faith in miracles of one kind or another," he said, "so we may as well pick the ones that make our lives better." I guess Pastor Ken minored in physics at Divinity School.

He suggested I pick up a copy of C.S. Lewis' *Mere Christianity*. I did so and found it to be brilliant. I read the book, read it again, and then read it for a third time. The historical Jesus, Lewis writes, claimed flat out to be the Son of God. Either he was crazy, or he was lying, or he was in fact the Son of God. There are no other options. Two thousand years later millions of people follow him. Are they worshipping a liar? A nutcase? As Lewis' logic wore me down, adding reason to the bit of faith I was already experiencing, my life began to change. Or, should I say, continued to change. Meeting Alley and falling in love with her had not been a coincidence. This I believed with all my heart.

I decided it was time to stop resisting and accept that I was a Christian. As I did so, a peace began to come over me, one which I had never known before. All my life I had trawled for happiness, caught and experienced it briefly, then let it slip away. As I started to feel loved by Jesus, I knew finally that the happiness could last.

XXII

O ne balmy evening on our porch overlooking the canal, we sat watching a pair of pelicans search for their dinner. They looked to me like old Jewish men. "Whadaya say, Morris, we eat a little bit of fish tonight?" Pelicans stop by the canals a few times a year, on their way to somewhere. Geese and cormorants do too, and the gorgeous egrets. Alley sat nursing a cup of Chamomile tea. Something was on her mind, I could tell.

"What's going on?" I asked.

"Alright. I've wanted to say something like this to you for a while."

"Like what?"

"You know you really hurt my feelings last night."

"What? How?"

"When Brian and Cynthia were here…after dinner, you just went in the bedroom and lay down and fell asleep."

"I hung out at the table for a while, and I figured they were your friends and they only really wanted to talk to you."

"It was rude, Orson, and it bothered me. You do that sort of thing. You're impatient. You write people off, instead of taking a little time to find out who they really are." I was startled. I guess I thought I had turned into the perfect Christian (forgetting that there'd only ever been one of those).

"So, while we're at it, what else bothers you about me?" (I was impatient to find out.)

"You're rude to people; I mean to strangers. Don't pay attention to them. I don't like it."

"That's just part of my charm, Al'."

"It's not, sweetheart. It doesn't charm me, and I don't think anybody else likes it either."

The third degree finally wound down, and Nagging Wyfe and I went to bed. I lay next to her, thinking. I guess I do tend to write people off sometimes. Was I becoming a holier-than-thou Christian? No, I'd been that way all my life. ("Never get to know the neighbors; they'll only want something from you": George Burrows.)

I've always tended to absorb things in my sleep; it's frequently how I learn. In the morning when we woke up, I took her in my arms. "I heard you last night, and I appreciate your having the guts to bring it up. I'll really try to be aware of it and ch, ch, ch... the *change* word."

She laughed and gave me a hug. "Thank you, Ors'." We got up and went about our day, Alley off to lunch with one of her friends, me cleaning out the storage shed. As I moved boxes around, I kept going over the things she'd said... and started to see more examples of what her complaints had been.

"Damn this being a Christian," I thought. "You can't get away with anything."

The next thought that came into my head was that I didn't want to get away with anything; I really did want to change. And it wasn't just about hurting Alley's feelings; it was about letting Christ into my life. Pretentiousness, pride, having to be *right...* all those things tended to shut Him out. Living in a way that invited Him in made me happy: so happy I felt like singing. Or making love to my wife. Or eating a cheeseburger.

———•———

We continued to worship at First Lutheran on Sundays. Alley decided she wanted to get baptized and make her conversion from Buddhism to Christianity official. She asked Pastor Ken to do the job in the ocean off Venice Beach. I went along, watched and took snapshots. It was moving. Afterwards, I began to feel a hankering for the same thing. The Pacific was as close as I was going to get to the River Jordan where John the Baptist had dunked the Boy, as I had come to call Him. Ken was happy to complete the family package. We picked a day, and the preacher agreed to connect up with us on the beach, near the jetty at the end of Venice Boulevard where he had done the deed with Alley. I put on my blue swimming trunks, a pair of sandals, and a nice Mexican shirt I never wear. Alley looked lovely in a sweet white cotton dress.

We walked down our canal heading for the ocean, and in ten minutes we were on the beach. I was carrying a little pile of towels. Pastor Ken was waiting for us, holding a towel of his own and his bible. He was wearing swimming trunks. "Nice legs," my wife said, and the preacher blushed. We continued toward the sea and stopped just as the sand was about to turn damp. Pastor Ken spread his towel. "Let's sit here for a minute," he said. "I'd like to read you a passage from the Good Book."

We all plopped down. Alley held my hand. The pastor leafed through the Bible and found the passage he was looking for. He told us it was from Mark. "And it came to pass that Jesus came from Nazareth and was baptized by John in the Jordan, and the Spirit descended upon Him like a dove. And a voice came from heaven: You are my beloved son in whom I am well pleased." Pastor Ken closed his bible. He talked a little more about the meaning of baptism and then stood up. "Alright, into the drink we go," he said. I kicked off my sandals and Alley and Ken shook off theirs. Our towels were in a little pile. Ken dropped his Bible on it. We waded on in. The water was cold. Alley held her dress up until the water reached her waist. Then she let it float. Ken stopped.

"I'm very proud to be doing this," he said. He put one hand on my shoulder and the other on the top of my head. "I baptize you in the name of the Father and of the Son and of the Holy Spirit." He pushed me down and under the water, then pulled me up right away. I was sopping wet and laughing. "Congratulations," he said. Alley gave me a big, squishy hug. Then, she hugged Pastor Ken.

"How do you feel?" she asked me.

"Re-born," I said. We all laughed, including me. But I meant it. We toweled off as best we could, then Pastor Ken took off for home and we walked back to the compound. We'd had a shower attached to the outside of one of the houses and we stood under it and let the warm water run over us, then dried off with fresh towels. I felt different, somehow. I was unsure how to describe the feeling. I could see why they call it born again. It was as if a fresh breeze were blowing through me. Jesus, my friend from New York, and I had made a bond.

Alley cooked a roast chicken and mashed potatoes that night, my favorite, and we ate by candlelight. She kept reaching across the table to take my hand. "We're really doing this," she said.

———————

A healing happened. Alley and my ex-wife took it upon themselves to befriend one another (the blessed mysteries of women). The still-beautiful dressmaker elected to forgive me and let go of her old hurt, for which I was deeply grateful. The kids no longer had to decide whose house to go to on birthdays and holidays; we all celebrate together.

———————

And yet another healing. As my marriage to Alley became stronger and our faith deepened, one thing still eluded me. I had not been able to get over my guilt about that phone call in the basement of the Continental Hotel in Cambridge. It had bothered my dreams for sixty-seven years. My father had died long since (I had been able to be with him in the last days, and had spoken at his funeral). But my mother lived on in me and laid a slight patina of sorrow over the happiest of times; and sometimes I knew it interfered with my ability to love my wife.

One morning I woke up, looked around the bedroom and realized that something important had changed, though I could not yet fathom what it was. The sun was peeking through the narrow space around the curtains in the French doors; the cat was sitting at the foot of the bed, staring at me with her usual baleful expression, one which said she couldn't believe I had not yet gotten up to feed her. But something was different. All at once, it dawned on me: the guilt I'd lived with my entire life over my mother's suicide was gone. It just wasn't there any more. I felt overwhelmed with love for her.

I had, a few years before, found in an old scrap book a group photo of her high school graduating class in Perkinsville, Vermont (1916). I had paid a photo shop to pull her image out and enlarge it. I'd framed the picture and hung it on the wall: a close-up of a pretty, vivacious seventeen year old, with a huge ribbon in her hair. A ribbon that size was clearly haute fashion back then. None of the other girls in her graduating class, probably farmers' daughters, had dared wear such a ribbon. Clearly, she had known she was beautiful, and was not afraid to flaunt it.

Tears filled my eyes as I thought of all that she had looked forward to: Cousin Cal was already governor of Massachusetts, her papa loved her to distraction, and she was the best looking girl in her class. How bright the future must have seemed. But she had, one night in the twenties, gone to a political meeting in Boston.

I got down on my knees next to the bed. "Thank you, God," I prayed out loud, "Thank you, thank you so much. And wherever she is, please let her be at peace... and know that her little boy loves her."

Which brings us, gentle reader, to present time. Alley and I have been married for twenty years. We keep working in the business, a blessing since we love what we do. I played a house husband on the last three seasons of Desperate Housewives. Alley was cast as Betty White's daughter on a soap opera, The Bold and the Beautiful. She's been on it for six years as of this writing and has come to love it. Our health is great, another blessing. I've had a couple of operations, no big deal. Every time I wake up with a little complaint, I take it as a chance to remind myself that I don't suffer from something really serious. (Whatever ache or pain I may experience, it doesn't hurt like spikes in the hands and feet.)

How blessed I am to have my family and friends and the air that I breathe. What a state of grace I'm in. And it's not because of anything I've done to earn it, but just because I am finally letting go of the absurd notion that I amount to anything. And as that happens, I find that I do, in fact, amount to a great deal: I am God's kid and He loves me. It was always free for the taking, and these days I'm taking it.

The Bible says that husband and wife become as one flesh. (Alley studies the Book; I find it rough going.) Together we grew, and became closer to our Maker in the process. I began to stop having an opinion about everyone; annoying types weren't so annoying anymore. And I realized I wasn't passing judgment as much on my own frailties either; I was actually beginning to like myself. So I'm "full of it" sometimes; I'm a man; it's my nature.

My view of life has changed. Success and the fame it brings has fallen into perspective. It's still fun to be recognized as a celebrity, like I was, for instance, after working with Charlie Sheen on his show. (Poor Charlie. I think he became possessed, and I don't just mean by drugs and hookers.) But nowadays it's fun to be recognized not because it pumps up my wretched little ego, but rather because it offers a chance to make contact with a fellow human whom I might otherwise never have met, but with whom I now have made a bond, however fleeting. Sometimes I come home smiling because somebody in the next car smiled at me.

I would find it difficult to explain this to a non-believer, but I have developed a one-on-one relationship with Jesus. This young Jewish man, who lived a long time ago in a part of the world I've never been to, has become my dearest and closest friend. I can't exactly see Him (though I did once, back in New York) but I feel his presence, and the touch of His hand on my shoulder when I'm going through a rough patch. When that happens, everything is different somehow, and the intense anxiety I've lived with all my life fades away. Paul (*that* Paul) called it "the peace that surpasses all understanding."

More than thirty years after the fact, I now realize what an extraordinary gift I received: an actual visit from Jesus Christ, in a New York apartment. It has remained for me, through all of my spiritual journey from skeptic to believer, a vividly real experience. There was never any doubt in my mind that on the two evenings in question, I had been in the physical presence of the living Christ; and if He was there then, He is surely here now, standing beside me as I type these words. Knowing that, how dare I not make every effort to become my best possible self. Why delude myself that what I see and feel and touch is all there is. It is there for me to enjoy and cherish and protect, but that's all it is. An infinitely greater and more loving reality exists all around me, right here and right now. My daily task, which I happily accept, is to make that reality mine.

I don't talk about God much to my grown kids, though I did do so to one of my daughters when my beloved son-in-law, Andrew, died suddenly and unexpectedly at the age of 43, leaving her with a passel of young children. When I held her in my arms and we cried together, I felt His comforting presence and wished with all my heart that my daughter could feel it. Maybe she will in time; I sense she may be starting to. I know He's there for her whether she is aware of it or not. (I can talk about the Boy to the grandchildren.)

———————

My prayer each day is "Thy will, not mine." By this, I mean I have discovered that what I *want* is quite frequently not what I *need*... so I am learning gratefully to accept what I *get*. Jesus knows what's best for me, knows what will make me feel content and satisfied. I feel like putting "Under New Management" on the marquee, as I start allowing His will to prevail. Trying to manage my own life, whether I consciously know it or not, is more exhausting and less profitable than running a candy store in the Bronx. What a relief it is to have Jesus beside me whispering in my ear to "relax and leave the driving to Us."

How do I respond to that whisper in my ear? I pray my thanks morning and evening, as per the instructions of Frankie from the sidewalk in front of the morning meeting. I converse with the dear Boy on and off throughout the day. When I'm driving, for instance, I may say, "Thank you for the green light, Lad." I don't mean by this that Jesus made the light turn green, or instructed the driver ahead of me to speed up so I could sneak through behind him just it was turning red. What I mean is that I'm overflowing with gratitude, and have an inexhaustible need to express it.

———————

Prayer is how I talk to Him. How does He talk to me? Sometimes through a sunset so thrillingly beautiful that Alley yells that I have to stop what I'm doing right now and come out onto the porch to take a look. But often by the way I feel when I have to decide whether to do one thing or another. I think about it and I just *know* which choice to make, that's all. That's the way he talks to me.

I have his picture, the one I bought at the Self Realization Center gift shop, on the wall of our bedroom, and I look at Him and smile with happiness. But sometimes I cry...tears actually roll down my cheeks, when I think about the way we treated Him and the way we treat one another. Somebody once said that if babies were strong enough, they'd kill us when they don't get their bottles on time. We seem to have to learn to be decent to one another. That's what Jesus helps me do these days.

———•••———

We changed churches and go to one called Pacific Crossroads. Rankin Wilbourne is a brilliant young pastor who preaches on Sundays to a couple of thousand of twenty or thirty year olds. (It's the only church we ever walked into where they said, "Oh, great, old people!") Alley brought her octogenarian bible teacher, Dottie Larson to hear him. She immediately left the church she'd been attending for fifty years and joined Rankins congregation. "He's the best preacher I've ever heard with the single exception of Billy Graham," she said. "And I've heard them all."

Pastor Ken and I are still closest of friends; we meet once a week for (buttered) bagels. Parker and I remain pen pals. My ninth grandchild was born in March of 2012 (the day after we buried dear Andrew). His name is Dallas Edward Andrew Bean! Eight of the nine grandkids live within a few minutes of me and, to my delight, are in and out of the house almost every day. If I'd known, I would have invested in Oreos and I'd be rich.

---·—·—·---

Sometime in the past, on the internet or somewhere, I read or saw or heard the following (forgive me for cribbing, whoever made it up): At my age, I find myself, from time to time, thinking about the end of things. And when my time does come, I hope to go the way my dear old grandfather did. Quietly in his sleep. Not *screaming* like the passengers in his car.

---·—·—·---

I am a grateful man. Grateful for being above ground, when statistically I might easily not be. Grateful for the California sky and the fig tree in the back yard. Grateful to the cat for not knocking me over when she walked between my legs this morning. Grateful for Folger's in my cup and for Mr. Thomas' decision to leave England and peddle his muffins here in American. Grateful for at long last feeling safe.

END

Thank Yous

Many thanks to my son Max and his partner John of Scout Idea Ranch for their invaluable help with the cover design. Ditto to my pals Richard Dry and Nancy Perkins for reading the manuscript and making excellent suggestions. Finally, I'm grateful to Heather and Staci of Balboa Press for making the publishing experience an easy pleasure.

Orson Bean was nominated for a SAG award for his performance in the film BEING JOHN MALKOVICH. He starred on Broadway for twenty years, winning a Theater World Award and a Tony nomination in the process. He appeared on The Tonight Show over 200 times, a hundred of them as substitute host. He continues to work in the theater and on TV,

Certain episodes in this tome have appeared, in different form, in other books I've written: Me and the Orgone, Too Much is not Enough and Mail for Mikey.